AMERICAN UNIVERSITY
NATIONAL SECURITY LAW BRIEF

Volume 8 • Number 1 • Spring 2018

Editorial Board

Editor in Chief
J. Chris White

Managing Editor
Annica Mae Mattus

Executive Editors
Eugene Mok
Casey Verrichia

Symposium Editor
Anthony Bjelke

Blog Editors
Prescott Heighton
Patrick Shaffer

Online Editor
Ryan Johnston

Senior Articles Editor
Daniel Wiltshire

Communications Editor
Cynthia Arellano

Articles Editor
Rachel Bauer

Consulting Editor
Kevin D. Reyes

Senior Staff

Josh Arons
Tammy Dang
Neah Evering
Victoria Garcia
Jen Goss
Sam Hamed
Ciprian Ivanof

Kara Kozikowksi
Kimberly Leon
Mohammed Loraoui
Jewel Massenberg
Ian Jones-Muniz
Samantha Nelson

Samuel Nicosia
Carly Nutall
Jaime Rosenberg
Dale Ton
Adam Vance
Sarah Watkins
Kate Youssouf

Junior Staff

Abigail Allardice
Leemor Banai
Alexis Bruce
John Burns
Samuel Cutler
Helina Daniel
Robert Davies

Joseph Epstein
Andrew Glenn
Ammar Hussain
Abigail Kittredge
Maria Latimer
Charles Lyons
Gabriella Marki
Halie Peacher

Alexa Potter
Maximilian Raileanu
Jamie Salazer
Lauren Stimpert
Amanda Sweitlik
Irving Vidal Terrazas
Frances Walizcek

AMERICAN UNIVERSITY
NATIONAL SECURITY LAW BRIEF

Volume 8 • Number 1 • Spring 2018

American University Washington College of Law
Washington, DC

NATIONAL SECURITY LAW BRIEF

American University National Security Law Brief, Volume 8, Number 1 (Spring 2018)

ISBN-13: 978-1986378475
ISBN-10: 1986378470

Founded in April 2009, the *American University National Security Law Brief* is the nation's first student-run law school publication to focus on the rapidly evolving field of national security law. The publication is published twice a year, with a complementary online component, and is edited and published by students at American University Washington College of Law.

The views and opinions expressed in the articles are solely those of the respective authors and do not necessarily represent those of the authors' employers, the publication, the editorial board, American University, or Washington College of Law

The brief welcomes manuscript submissions on relevant topics in national security law and policy

Copyright © 2018 by the American University National Security Law Brief
All rights reserved. No part of this publication may be reproduced without prior written permission from the brief.

For more information about the publication, submissions, or permissions, please visit the brief's website

Website: nationalsecuritylawbrief.com
Twitter: @AUNatlSecLaw
Facebook: @AUNatlSecLaw
LinkedIn: linkedin.com/company/AUNatlSecLaw

Bluebook abbreviation: AM. U. NAT'L SEC. L. BRIEF

American University National Security Law Brief
Washington College of Law
American University
4300 Nebraska Avenue NW
Washington, DC 20016

Cover and design by Kevin D. Reyes (consulting editor) (kevindreyes.com)
Printed by CreateSpace, an Amazon Company

AMERICAN UNIVERSITY
NATIONAL SECURITY LAW BRIEF

Volume 8 • Number 1 • Spring 2018

Contents

1   Editorial Note

3   The Posse Comitatus Act and the Fourth Amendment's Exclusionary Rule
     Lieutenant Colonel Patrick Walsh and Paul Sullivan

43   How Cybersecurity Regulation for the Smart Grid Could Upset the Current Balance of Federal and State Jurisdiction in Electricity Regulation
     Cynthia Anderson

Editorial Note

Dear readers,

This issue of the eighth volume of the *American University National Security Law Brief* spotlights key issues emerging from the Fourth Amendment's exclusionary rule and emerging Smart Grid influence on electricity regulation. The following articles cut to the core of these issues through penetrating legal analysis and hard-hitting commentary.

The U.S. Military can often be feared by the public when taking action on U.S. soil, but also recognized for its unique ability to respond in a timely, well organized, and efficient manner to domestic unrest or disaster. In our first article, Lieutenant Colonel Patrick Walsh and Paul Sullivan dissect the common misapplication of the exclusionary rule and the Posse Comitatus Act in excluding evidence during criminal trials. The authors argue three key points: (1) the misuse of the exclusionary rule when applied to domestic law enforcement activity; (2) the misuse of the military inside the United States; and (3) the exclusionary rule should not be the mechanism used in attempts to deter the use of the military for law enforcement activities. Ultimately, this article concludes that while both the exclusionary rule and Posse Comitatus Act are essential in protecting civil liberties and preventing overreach by government officials, violations of the Posse Comitatus Act should not fall under the exclusionary rule.

The United States produces the second largest gigawatt hours of any country, and this production is essential not just to the daily lives of Americans, but to the global economy. As more and more facets of life are "electrified" and the global economy continues to interweave, the importance of adequate cybersecurity protecting America's Smart Grid will become paramount. Cynthia Anderson's article breaks down the legal issues surrounding the debate between increasing federal regulations to establish industry-wide cybersecurity standards and maintaining state autonomy in interstate transmission and wholesale sales. The author argues that due to increasing interconnectivity across state lines as part of the Smart Grid, the notion that a power disruption can be considered local is no longer realistic. Further, the article presents the need for a combined effort that utilizes federally mandated standards forcing action at the local level, while preserving the ability for local agencies to react to newly discovered vulnerabilities through the implementation of the latest emerging technology.

Mahalo,

J. Chris White

The Posse Comitatus Act and the Fourth Amendment's Exclusionary Rule

Lieutenant Colonel Patrick Walsh and Paul Sullivan[*]

I. INTRODUCTION

The United States has, throughout its history, continually called upon the U.S. military to deploy inside the United States to respond to disasters, to protect citizens in times of war, and even to perform acts of law enforcement during civil unrest. At the same time, Americans have a long-standing and inherent distrust of the use of the military on U.S. soil, particularly for law enforcement activities. These two competing interests—to use the military in times of need but restrict its domestic use for law enforcement—have created a mix of court cases that apply different tests to determine when the military has exceeded its legal authority to operate inside the United States.

---

[*] **Patrick Walsh** is the legal curriculum branch chief at the Federal Law Enforcement Training Center, where he supervises and teaches law to aspiring federal and military law enforcement officers. He received an LLM from the University of Virginia School of Law, a second LLM from the U.S. Army Judge Advocate General's Legal Center and School, and a JD from the University of California, Berkeley, School of Law. Lieutenant Colonel Walsh is also a judge advocate in the United States Army Reserve and assigned as an adjunct professor at the U.S. Army Judge Advocate General's Legal Center and School.

Paul Sullivan is the legal division administrative branch chief at the Federal Law Enforcement Training Center, where he supervises and teaches Fourth Amendment law to aspiring federal and military law enforcement officers. He received his JD from Creighton University School of Law. Mr. Sullivan has served as a State Department Justice Advisor in conflict and post-conflict nations. Prior to attending law school, Mr. Sullivan was a police officer for the City of Leawood, Kansas.

The court's primary tool for restricting the use of the military as domestic law enforcement is to use the Fourth Amendment's exclusionary rule to suppress evidence gathered in violation of the restrictions on the domestic use of the military. Recently, the Supreme Court has reevaluated and restricted the application of the exclusionary rule. The Court has emphasized that the exclusionary rule should be judiciously applied to suppress evidence of criminal activity. Courts need to follow this recent Supreme Court guidance and recognize that the exclusionary rule should not be used to suppress evidence derived from the domestic use of the military.

This article will examine both the use of the military inside the United States and the recent restrictions on applying the exclusionary rule to deter government violations of law. The article will highlight where these areas of the law intersect in the courts—when criminal defendants seek the application of the exclusionary rule to exclude evidence gathered while the military was engaged in an impermissible act of law enforcement. By examining recent military operations inside the United States and looking at the evolving development of the exclusionary rule, there is a clear answer: the Fourth Amendment's exclusionary rule is misused when courts apply it to the military's domestic law enforcement activity.

Section II will examine the development of the use—and misuse—of the military inside the United States to conduct law enforcement activity. Section III will explore the development of the exclusionary rule, including the recent Supreme Court opinions that have emphasized the exclusionary rule's limited purpose. Section IV will examine the recent judicial applications of the exclusionary rule to law enforcement activity by the military, and review how the lower courts are ruling in a manner that is inconsistent with current Supreme Court guidance on the exclusionary rule. Section V will synthesize these two conflicts and explain how the exclusionary rule is an ineffective and sometimes counterproductive mechanism to deter law enforcement activity by the military.

II. DOMESTIC MILITARY OPERATIONS AND LAW ENFORCEMENT

Throughout its history, the United States has had a complicated relationship with the use of the military for domestic law enforcement. Some of the primary complaints against Great Britain that preceded the Declaration of Independence involved the use of the British military inside the Colonies.[1] Despite this unease, the U.S. Constitution anticipates and permits the domestic use of the military.[2] Congress sanctioned the use of the military to enforce the law early on in U.S. history.[3] The controversy continued during and after the American Civil War, when Congress initially reaffirmed the domestic use of the military to enforce the law and later criminalizing use of the military for domestic law enforcement.[4] Exploring the tension about the need to use the military for law enforcement and the concerns over doing so will be explored in this section.

A. The Declaration of Independence, the Articles of Confederation, and the U.S. Constitution

In the years before the drafting of the Constitution and the passing of the Bill of Rights, America struggled with the role of military in domestic affairs.[5] American colonists objected to the use of the British Army to enforce British law and supplant the civil law of the

---

[1] THE DECLARATION OF INDEPENDENCE paras. 13, 16 (U.S. 1776); David McCullough, John Adams 65 (2001); Sean J. Kealy, *Reexamining the Posse Comitatus Act: Toward a Right to Civil Law Enforcement*, 21 YALE L. & POL'Y REV. 383, 389–92 (2003).

[2] U.S. CONST. art. I, § 8; *id.* art. II, § 2; *id.* art. IV, § 4.

[3] Calling Forth Act of 1792, ch. 28, 1 Stat. 264 (repealed 1795); Militia Act of 1795, ch. 36, 1 Stat. 424 (current version at 10 U.S.C. §§ 331–35 (2000)).

[4] *See* Gary Felicetti & John Luce, *The Posse Comitatus Act: Setting the Record Straight on 124 Years of Mischief and Misunderstanding Before Any More Damage Is Done*, 175 MIL. L. REV. 86, 95–96 (2003) (explaining that the sheriff's power to use the military in law enforcement pre-dated the Framers' concern over centralized power at the time the Constitution was drafted).

[5] THE DECLARATION OF INDEPENDENCE paras. 13, 16 (U.S. 1776); *see* U.S. CONST. amend. III; ARTICLES OF CONFEDERATION of 1781, arts. VI, VII, IX; Laird v. Tatum, 408 U.S. 1, 22–23 (1972); David E. Engdahl, *Soldiers, Riots, and Revolution: The Law and History of Military Troops in Civil Disorders*, 57 IOWA L. REV. 1 (1971); Clarence I. Meeks, III, *Illegal Law Enforcement: Aiding Civil Authorities in Violation of the Posse Comitatus Act*, 70 MIL. L. REV. 83, 86 (1975).

Colonies.⁶ The Articles of Confederation, the Constitution, and the amendments to the Constitution included law that restricted and limited the power and use of the military.⁷ At the same time, the early Congresses authorized presidents to use the military on U.S. soil to battle insurrectionists, respond to threats, and even enforce some federal laws.⁸ The first leaders of America struggled, much as today's leaders have, to define the proper use of the military for domestic activities.⁹

i. The Declaration of Independence and Its Objections to the Military as a Law Enforcement Body

Colonists who moved from Great Britain to the New World brought with them ideas that the military should not be used for domestic law enforcement.¹⁰ Consequently, these colonists believed they were being treated unjustly when King George sent the British Army into the colonial cities to enforce British law and order.¹¹ The British Army occupied the city of Boston from 1768 to 1770 to exert control over the unruly colonists and enforce British taxes.¹² The perceived injustice of being subject to military enforcement of civil law increased opposition to the British monarchy. Rather than decrease opposition, the employment of British troops in law enforcement actually led to an increase in violence between occupying British forces and the colonists.¹³

---

⁶ Kealy, *supra note* 1, at 389–92.

⁷ THE DECLARATION OF INDEPENDENCE paras. 13, 16 (U.S. 1776); *see* U.S. CONST. amend. III; ARTICLES OF CONFEDERATION of 1781, arts. VI, VII, IX; *Laird*, 408 U.S. at 22–23; Engdahl, *supra note* 5, at 1; Meeks, *supra note* 5, at 86 (discussing the Framers' concerns over military involvement in the lives of civilians absent civilian control).

⁸ Calling Forth Act of 1792; Militia Act of 1795; Act of Apr. 30, 1790, ch. 10, 1 Stat. 119; Act of Sept. 29, 1789, ch. 25, 1 Stat. 96.

⁹ *See generally* BENNETT MILTON RICH, PRESIDENTS AND CIVIL DISORDER 21, 25–26 (1941) (discussing the use of troops to quell Fries's Rebellion).

¹⁰ *See* Engdahl, *supra note* 5, at 1 (describing the role of due process in preventing the use of military force in suppressing civil disorders); *see also* FAITH THOMPSON, MAGNA CARTA: ITS ROLE IN THE MAKING OF THE ENGLISH CONSTITUTION, 1300–1629, at 68 (1948); MATTHEW HALE, THE HISTORY OF THE COMMON LAW OF ENGLAND 49 (2d ed. 1716).

¹¹ Kealy, *supra note* 1, at 390.

¹² *Id.* at 389–92.

¹³ MCCULLOUGH, *supra note* 1, at 65.

On March 5, 1770, when British troops and colonists confronted each other amid protests in Boston, the troops fired, killing five men.[14] This use of British troops as a "force of uniformed peace-keepers, or policemen," which resulted in the death of protesters, came to be known as the "Boston Massacre."[15] Despite the public outcry following the deaths, British troops continued to patrol the streets of the Colonies and enforce British taxes and regulations through the 1770s.[16]

Six years after the Boston Massacre, Thomas Jefferson included grievances in the Declaration of Independence that cited the misuse of the British troops for law enforcement.[17] Jefferson's list of grievances included the keeping of "standing armies" in times of peace, rendering the British military "independent of and superior to the Civil power," and "quartering of large bodies of armed troops among us."[18] These concerns were remembered when the founding republic established its first government with the passage of the Articles of Confederation.

ii. *The Articles of Confederation and Their Restrictions on the Military*

The Articles of Confederation—in establishing the first national government for the United States—reflected the Founding Fathers' concerns over the domestic use of the military.[19] The Articles required that, in peacetime, the Armed Forces must be limited only to the size that was absolutely necessary for the national defense and that the military must always be subject to civilian control.[20] The Articles favored the traditional state militias (with part-time soldiers instead of professionals) and with officers appointed by and beholden to the

---

[14] *Id.* at 65–66; HILLER B. ZOBEL, THE BOSTON MASSACRE 135 (Easton Press 1987) (1971).
[15] ZOBEL, *supra* note 14, at 135.
[16] *See* Meeks, *supra* note 5, at 86.
[17] THE DECLARATION OF INDEPENDENCE paras. 13, 16 (U.S. 1776).
[18] *Id.*
[19] *See* ARTICLES OF CONFEDERATION of 1781, arts. VI, VII, IX (establishing civilian control of the military and limiting military size based on national defense needs).
[20] *Id.*

States for their position.[21] These restrictions along with a weak central government were insufficient to protect the nation and the Founding Fathers convened again to create an improved and stronger central government.

iii. The U.S. Constitution and Its Regulation of the Military

The U.S. Constitution granted broader powers to the federal government to raise and maintain a military, but it also maintained prior safeguards that regulated the use of the military inside the United States.[22] During the Constitutional Convention, some delegates raised concerns about permitting a standing army, but the majority overruled these concerns.[23] The Constitution granted Congress the power to raise a standing army, but imposed safeguards on it from both the legislative and executive branch.[24] The new Constitution also gave the military a domestic role, to "suppress Insurrections" and, perhaps, to protect against "domestic Violence."[25] These constitutional provisions raised some concerns about the misuse of the military inside the United States, and states called for a "Bill of Rights" to amend the Constitution to address these concerns.[26]

The Bill of Rights created additional restrictions on the domestic use of the military to address the fears of misuse.[27] The Second Amendment guaranteed a well-regulated militia loyal to the states, and the right for citizens to maintain arms.[28] The Third Amendment

---

[21] *Id.*
[22] U.S. CONST. art. I, § 8; *id.* art, II, § 2.
[23] ROBERT W. COAKLEY, THE ROLE OF FEDERAL MILITARY FORCES IN DOMESTIC DISORDER, 1789–1878, at 4–12 (1988); DANIEL A. FARBER & SUZANNA SHERRY, A HISTORY OF THE AMERICAN CONSTITUTION 140, 180–81 (1990).
[24] U.S. CONST. art. I, § 8; *id.* art. II, § 2. (granting Congress the power to review military appropriations, the power to raise the standing army, the power to declare war, and making the military subordinate to the President).
[25] U.S. CONST. art. I, § 8, cl. 15; *id.* art. IV, § 4.
[26] *See* THE FEDERALIST No. 8, at 122–23 (Alexander Hamilton) (Benjamin Fletcher Wright ed., 1961); THE FEDERALIST No. 41, at 296 (James Madison) (Benjamin Fletcher Wright ed., 1961).
[27] Laird v. Tatum, 408 U.S. 1, 22–23 (1972).
[28] U.S. CONST. amend. II; *see also Laird*, 408 U.S. at 22–23.

addressed the very concerns that inflamed Boston residents at the time of the Boston Massacre, prohibiting the housing of federal troops in citizens' homes against their wishes.[29] These restrictions directly addressed the serious concerns Americans had about the misuse of the British Army before American independence. The amendments assuaged some of the concerns about using the military domestically, because the early Congress often used the military to enforce federal law.[30]

After the Constitution was ratified, Congress assembled and began exercising its legislative authority and began to permit the domestic use of the military. First, Congress authorized the President to call the militia to protect the frontier from "hostile incursions of the Indians."[31] Next, Congress enabled the militias to respond to invasion, insurrection, and obstruction of the laws.[32] These acts permitted the President to call forth the militia for a limited time, when "the laws of the United States shall be opposed, or the execution thereof obstructed . . ."[33] The President had authority to act only after he issued a proclamation commanding the "insurgents" to disperse.[34]

iv. The Use of the Military by the Founding Fathers

President George Washington first used this "calling forth" authority to suppress the Whiskey Rebellion in Western Pennsylvania, an insurrection that rebelled against federal government taxes on the production of whiskey.[35] In activating the state militia to suppress the

---

[29] U.S. CONST. amend. III; *see also Laird*, 408 U.S. at 22–23.

[30] *See* Calling Forth Act of 1792, ch. 28, § 2, 1 Stat. 264 (repealed 1795) (granting the President authority to use state militias to defend against domestic threats).

[31] Act of Apr. 30, 1790, ch. 10, 1. Stat. 96; *Id.* § 16, 1 Stat. 119, 121 (repealed 1795) (regulating the military establishment of the United States).

[32] Militia Act of 1795, ch. 36, 1 Stat. 424 (current version at 10 U.S.C. §§ 331–35 (2000)); Calling Forth Act of 1792.

[33] Calling Forth Act of 1792 § 2.

[34] *Id.* § 3.

[35] *See* 3 ANNALS OF CONG. 1411 (1794) (Gales and Seaton 1855) (proclamation of President Washington, Aug. 7, 1794); *id.* 1413 (proclamation of President Washington, Sept. 25, 1794) (discussing the implications of the proclamations and their use during the Whiskey Rebellion); STEVEN R. BOYD, THE WHISKEY REBELLION: PAST AND PRESENT PERSPECTIVES 123 (1985); 5 JAMES D. RICHARDSON, A COMPILATION OF THE MESSAGES

insurrection, Congress and the President understood that the military was there only to assist civilian power in enforcing the law, not to supplant local authority.[36] The civilian federal law enforcement and the civilian federal courts maintained primary authority to enforce the tax and prosecute offenders.

The Founding Fathers who ratified the new Constitution continued to use the military inside the United States without significant objection.[37] Each use was in support of the civilian authorities and sometimes directly supported law enforcement. The military was used by President John Adams to suppress the 1799 Fries Rebellion with little objection.[38] The military arrested the leader, John Fries, and other conspirators, and turned them over to civil authorities for prosecution.[39] President Thomas Jefferson called out federal troops to enforce the Embargo Act, a tax opposed by Vermont traders.[40] Congress ratified the action by amending the Embargo Act to permit the use of federal troops to enforce it.[41]

In each of these instances, there was general support for using the military to enforce domestic law. However, each instance involved the President calling forth the military only with the approval of Congress. The military acted to enforce civilian law, but did so in support of the civilian law enforcement, and did not supplant or usurp civilian authority. Therefore, the early leaders of America both understood the dangers posed by using the military as a domestic enforcer

---

AND PAPERS OF THE PRESIDENTS 158–62 (1896); THOMAS P. SLAUGHTER, THE WHISKEY REBELLION: FRONTIER EPILOGUE TO THE AMERICAN REVOLUTION 165, 196–97 (1986).

[36] *See* Engdahl, *supra* note 5, at 49–50 (explaining the doctrinal role of military troops in assisting in the enforcement of civilian law).

[37] *See generally* FREDERICK T. WILSON, FEDERAL AID IN DOMESTIC DISTURBANCES, 1787–1903, S. Doc. No. 57-209, at 38, 51, 57 (1903) (providing an overview of the use of federal troops in providing aid during domestic disturbances from 1787 to 1922 and specific instances of use by several early presidents).

[38] RICH, *supra* note 9, at 21, 25–26.

[39] President John Adams, Proclamation of March 12, 1799, *reprinted in* WILSON, *supra* note 37, at 43.

[40] Embargo Act of 1807, ch. 5, 2 Stat. 451 (repealed 1809) (calling for an embargo on all ships and vessels in the ports and harbors of the United States).

[41] Act of Dec. 22, 1807, ch. 5, 2 Stat. 506, 510 (repealed 1809) (authorizing the use of federal troops in enforcement of the Embargo Act).

of the law, and the need to still use the military on occasion to enforce domestic law.

Prior to the Civil War, the federal government used the military domestically for other purposes. The military was called upon to prevent U.S. flagged vessels from violating U.S. neutrality in European wars,[42] to detain and seize illegally armed vessels preparing to fight in foreign wars,[43] to defeat the conspiracy of Aaron Burr,[44] and for other purposes.[45] Each of these involved the use of the military to enforce civil law, but the military was enforcing laws that seem to fit comfortably in the military's primary mission to defend the nation. There was little concern about the use of the military in these circumstances.

Concerns about using the military domestically increased dramatically before and after the Civil War, when civilian authorities began to use the military as a *posse comitatus*[46] and in other ways to enforce civil law that was not related to the military's primary purpose. The military—or to be more specific—the Union Army, began to play a greater role in the enforcement of the law, and often against the will of the local population. The tensions at the founding of America regarding the use of the military to enforce laws returned.

---

[42] *See generally* Act of June 5, 1794, ch. 50, 1 Stat. 381 (repealed 1818) (prohibiting U.S. citizens from joining in or supporting military activities of foreign states); CHARLES G. FENWICK, THE NEUTRALITY LAWS OF THE UNITED STATES 15–18 (1913) (describing early neutrality statutes and the U.S. position on avoiding entanglements in foreign wars).

[43] Act of June 5, 1794, § 7, 1 Stat. 381, 384.

[44] President Thomas Jefferson, Message to Congress on the Burr Conspiracy (Jan. 22, 1807), *in* AMERICAN PRESIDENCY PROJECT, http://www.presidency.ucsb.edu/ws/?pid=65721; *see also* WILSON, *supra* note 37, at 48.

[45] *See* Proclamation No. 194, 16 Stat. 1136 (Oct. 12, 1870) (prohibiting citizens of the United States from engaging in military enterprises against countries with whom the United States is at peace); FENWICK, *supra*, note 42, at 15–18 (proposing to stop U.S. aid to Canadian rebels); RICHARDSON, *supra* note 35, at 7–8 (discussing actions taken to stop an expedition preparing to attack Cuba); WILSON, *supra* note 37, at 51–53 (discussing U.S. actions to halt militant activity on the Canadian border).

[46] *Posse comitatus* is discussed in detail in the next section. It generally refers to the power of a law enforcement officer to compel the assistance of citizens to help the officer enforce the law. *See infra* Section II.B.i.

B. Posse Comitatus, the Civil War and Reconstruction

The domestic use of the military began to change in the decades prior to the Civil War. While the Founding Fathers approved the use of the military domestically for law enforcement activities like enforcing neutrality and suppressing riots that oppose the taxation systems, the early history predominately involved the President or Congress directing the military to act.[47] On some occasions, like the Whiskey Rebellion, the President actually led the soldiers in the domestic operation.[48] As the Civil War grew closer, the decision to use the military for law enforcement was delegated to lower and lower levels of government. Federal and state officials in local communities began to call soldiers to assist local law enforcement under a common-law doctrine called posse comitatus.[49]

i. Posse Comitatus

Common law authorized county sheriffs to require able-bodied men to assist them in arresting fugitives and in performing other law enforcement activities.[50] Prior to American independence, state and county law enforcement officials in the Colonies continued to exert this British common-law authority.[51] When Congress created federal marshals, the federal equivalent of a county sheriff, Congress granted

---

[47] *See* RICH, *supra* note 9, at 21, 25–26; SLAUGHTER, *supra* note 35, 165, 196–97 (1986); Engdahl, *supra* note 5, at 49–50 (explaining the doctrinal role of military troops in assisting in the enforcement of civilian law).

[48] HENRY M. BRACKENRIDGE, HISTORY OF THE WESTERN INSURRECTION IN WESTERN PENNSYLVANIA, COMMONLY CALLED THE WHISKEY INSURRECTION (1859); WILLIAM FINDLEY, HISTORY OF THE INSURRECTION IN THE FOUR WESTERN COUNTIES OF PENNSYLVANIA 195 (1796); WILSON, *supra* note 37, at 32–34 (discussing U.S. actions to halt militant activity on the Canadian border).

[49] *See* Felicetti & Luce, *supra* note 4, at 95–96 (discussing the lack of an explicit limit on the ability of local governments to call upon soldiers for law enforcement).

[50] *See id.*

[51] *See* United States v. Hart, 545 F. Supp. 470, 472 (D.N.D. 1982) (holding that common law permits a sheriff to organize a *posse*); *see also* WILLIAM BLACKSTONE, COMMENTARIES ON THE LAWS OF ENGLAND, 817 (George Sharswood ed., 1893) (stating that a sheriff has *posse comitatus* power to require citizens to assist in the arrest of felons).

them this common-law authority of posse comitatus.[52] As a result, there were federal law enforcement officers in every federal district who could require all local citizens to assist them in enforcing federal law. This authority to call upon private citizens to form a *posse* was without controversy. However, the controversy returned when marshals and sheriffs began to use this authority to require not just civilians, but also federal troops and state militias, to assist in enforcing federal law.[53]

As the practice of using the military to support law enforcement grew, Congress began to legislate the use of the posse comitatus to enforce the law.[54] The Fugitive Slave Act was one such law.[55] Pursuant to the act, owners of escaped slaves were entitled to an arrest warrant for the slave.[56] Federal marshals were required to execute these warrants, and the marshal could require the assistance of "all good citizens" in the county.[57] The act did not specifically state that the marshal could require the assistance of soldiers, but it also did not prohibit the use of the military to assist civilian police.[58] After fierce opposition to the law occurred in Boston and elsewhere, the President issued a proclamation requiring the military to assist federal marshals who were executing federal warrants for former slaves who had fled to a state that prohibited slavery.[59] The Secretary of War affirmed this proclamation with an order to federal troops to assist marshals if needed.[60]

---

[52] *See* Judiciary Act of 1789, ch. 20, § 27, 1 Stat. 73, 87 (granting marshals the authority to appoint deputies and command assistance); *see also* Calling Forth Act, ch. 28, § 9, 1 Stat. 264, 265 (1792) (repealed 1795) (stating that marshals have same powers under federal law as sheriffs have under state law).

[53] *See* CONG. GLOBE, 34th Cong., 1st & 2d Sess. 1757 (1856) (proposing legislation and discussion by Congress of local authorities to use the military as a posse comitatus).

[54] *See* Fugitive Slave Act of 1850, ch. 60, § 5, 9 Stat. 462, 463 (repealed 1864).

[55] *Id.*

[56] *Id.*

[57] *Id.*

[58] *See id.* at 462–63.

[59] Proclamation of Feb. 18, 1851, 9 Stat. 1006 (President Millard Fillmore's proclamation requiring the military to assist with enforcement of the act); WILSON, *supra* note 37, at 62.

[60] WILSON, *supra* note 37, at 62.

Even the Senate Judiciary Committee agreed that federal marshals could use the military as a posse comitatus.[61]

The U.S. Attorney General concurred in the use of the military to enforce federal, state, and local law. Attorney General Caleb Cushing issued an opinion stating that soldiers stationed in a county were part of the posse comitatus and were required to assist law enforcement.[62] Armed with the concurrence of the President, Congress, the Secretary of War, and the Attorney General, law enforcement began robust use of the military to enforce the law, especially laws that were unpopular with the local community.[63] The military chain of command could be relied on to enforce unpopular laws even when local police officers might use their discretion and decline to enforce unpopular criminal laws in their jurisdiction. This expanded use of the military to enforce unpopular laws appeared to be partisan—used by one political party to enforce laws unpopular with an opposing party.[64] Since the military was not supposed to favor one political party over another, this use of the military appeared inappropriate.[65] The use, or misuse, of the military to enforce civilian law heightened during, and after, the Civil War.

ii. Posse Comitatus and the Civil War

The exigencies brought on by the Civil War led to an expansion of the use of the military to enforce civil law.[66] In 1861, Congress authorized the President to use the state militias or federal army when it was not practicable to enforce the law through civilian law enforcement.[67] Before the Civil War, the military could be used as a posse comitatus, or otherwise to enforce the law, only if they remained subordinate to

---

[61] COAKLEY, *supra* note 23, at 130; S. REP. NO. 31-320 (1851).
[62] 6 Op. Att'y Gen. 466, 473 (1854); *see also* COAKLEY, *supra* note 23, at 133–37.
[63] RICHARDSON, *supra* note 35, at 358; *see also* 9 Op. Att'y Gen. 516, 522 (1860).
[64] *See supra* note 53, at 1813 (1856) (proposed legislation and discussion by Congress disapproving of the use of the military in Kansas as a posse comitatus).
[65] *Id.*
[66] *See* Kealy, *supra* note 1, at 393.
[67] Act of July 29, 1861, ch. 25, § 8, 12 Stat. 281.

civil authority.[68] As the Civil War developed, the military began to assert authority to enforce law without deference to civil law enforcement. As the Union Army began to win battles and secure land in secessionist states, it began to reassert the law of the union and engage in all areas of law enforcement.

iii. Posse Comitatus and Reconstruction

After the war ended, the Union Army took control of the government of some of the defeated Southern states.[69] Under their own direction, the military kept public order, enforced taxes on whiskey production, arrested members of the Klu Klux Klan, and guarded polling places.[70] The military even seized several state legislatures and became involved in local political matters and resolved local disputes between whites and former slaves.[71] The most controversial use of the military was to protect polling stations in the highly disputed election between Samuel J. Tilden and Rutherford B. Hayes.[72]

Hayes won very close elections in South Carolina, Louisiana, and Florida.[73] In those same states, President Ulysses Grant ordered the Union Army to assist federal marshals in protecting the polling stations.[74] Some argued the military's assistance and presence at the polls helped sway the election in these states, and the overall presidency to Hayes.[75] A dispute over who won the election ensued.[76] Ultimately,

---

[68] 9 Op. Att'y Gen. 516, 522 (1860).
[69] Reconstruction Act of 1867, ch. 153, 14 Stat. 428 (creating the military districts to govern defeated states).
[70] James P. O'Shaugnhessy, Note, *The Posse Comitatus Act: Reconstruction Politics Reconsidered*, 13 AM. CRIM. L. REV. 703, 704–10 (1976).
[71] Kealy, *supra* note 1, at 393.
[72] *See* 5 CONG. REC. 2117 (1877) (remarks of Rep. Banning claiming that soldiers did the Hayes campaign's "dirty work").
[73] *Id.*
[74] *Id.*
[75] *See* JEFFREY ROGERS HUMMEL, EMANCIPATING SLAVES, ENSLAVING FREE MEN: A HISTORY OF THE AMERICAN CIVIL WAR 321 (1996) (arguing that the Army preferred Hayes and therefore helped sway the election); *see also* H.W.C. Furman, *Restrictions Upon the Use of the Army Imposed by the Posse Comitatus Act*, 27 MIL. L. REV. 85, 94 (1960).
[76] HUMMEL, *supra* note 75, at 321.

Congress resolved the disputed election, and Hayes secured the presidency the day before Inauguration Day.[77] As a concession to his opponents, President Hayes agreed to withdraw troops from the South, and he signed a law criminalizing the use of the Army as a posse comitatus.[78] Congress and the President then began a process to restrict the use of the military in domestic affairs, especially domestic law enforcement at the order of local officials.

C. Restoring Limits on the Military by Criminalizing Posse Comitatus

During Reconstruction, southern legislators objected to the intrusive and prolonged use of the military for domestic law enforcement. The military had far exceeded its historic domestic responsibilities. Local officials, not the President, had the ability to require the military to assist in enforcing domestic law at the local level. This local military intrusion into criminal-law enforcement went beyond the expectations and desires of Americans, and in 1878, Congress passed the Posse Comitatus Act to restore the limitations on the ability of local officials to the military to arrest offenders and enforce the law.[79]

The Posse Comitatus Act passed with little fanfare in an appropriations bill in 1878.[80] The current version of the statute reads:

> Whoever, except in cases and under circumstances expressly authorized by the Constitution or Act of Congress, willfully uses any part of the Army or the Air Force as a posse comitatus or otherwise to execute the laws shall be fined under this title or imprisoned not more than two years, or both.[81]

---

[77] Kealy, *supra* note 1, at 394.
[78] HUMMEL, *supra* note 75, at 321; Kealy, *supra* note 1, at 394.
[79] *See* Posse Comitatus Act, §15, 20 Stat. 152 (1878) (codified as amended at 18 U.S.C. § 1385 (2016)).
[80] *See id.*
[81] *See* 18 U.S.C. § 1385. The early version was substantially similar, but it was later amended to include the Air Force after it was separated from the Army and became its own branch of the Armed Forces. Presumably, Congress initially excluded the Navy and the Marine Corps because they did not pose the same risk of domestic law enforcement as the Army. Later, Congress passed a separate law requiring the

The law clearly prohibits federal marshals and county sheriffs from calling military units into service as a *posse comitatus*.[82] It also prohibits the use of the Army to "execute the laws," implying a broader scope to the prohibition.[83] The act is also a criminal statute—violation of which is a felony.[84] However, there are no reported convictions of soldiers, airmen, or anyone else for violating the act.[85] Despite this, numerous state and federal courts have issued opinions on the act.[86] These cases routinely involve a defendant who is trying to suppress evidence in his criminal prosecution because the military's involvement violated the Posse Comitatus Act.[87] The court decisions create differing and inconsistent rulings on what constitutes a Posse Comitatus Act violation and what the consequence of that violation should be.[88] Reviewing these cases demonstrate that the military still acts as a posse comitatus and/or is used to execute the laws in violation of the Posse Comitatus Act, even though no one is prosecuted.[89]

There is a reason why there have been repeated violations of the Posse Comitatus Act but no prosecutions. A tension still exists

---

Department of Defense to issue regulations restricting the Navy and the Marine Corps from engaging in improper domestic law enforcement. *See* 10 U.S.C. § 375 (2011).

[82] *See* WILLIAM WINTHROP, MILITARY LAW AND PRECEDENTS 867 (2d ed. 1920).

[83] *See* 18 U.S.C. § 1385 (2016).

[84] *See id.*

[85] Furman, *supra* note 75, at 94 (discussing reports that, in 1879, two Army officers were indicted in Texas for providing U.S. marshals with troops to enforce revenue laws, but there is no record that they were convicted); *see also* G. NORMAN LIEBER, OFFICE OF THE JUDGE ADVOCATE, U.S. WAR DEP'T, DOC. NO. 64, THE USE OF THE ARMY IN AID OF THE CIVIL POWER 28 n.1 (1898); Matthew Carlton Hammond, Note, *The Posse Comitatus Act: A Principle in Need of Renewal*, 75 Wash. U. L.Q. 953, 961 (1997).

[86] *See* Hammond, *supra* note 85, at 953, 961, 965–67.

[87] *See* Casper v. United States, 430 U.S. 970 (1977); United States v. Dreyer, 804 F.3d 1266 (9th Cir. 2015) (*en banc*); United States v. Red Feather, 541 F.2d 1275 (8th Cir. 1976); United States v. Red Feather, 392 F. Supp. 916 (D.S.D. 1975), *aff'd*, 541 F.2d 1275 (8th Cir. 1976); People v. Burden, 288 N.W.2d 392 (Mich. Ct. App. 1979) (applying the exclusionary rule to a drug investigation in which a member of the U.S. Air Force participated with the approval of his commander), *rev'd*, 303 N.W.2d 444 (Mich. 1981); Taylor v. State, 645 P.2d 522 (Okla. Crim. App. 1982) (applying the exclusionary rule for a Posse Comitatus Act violation as a result of a military police officer's active participation in a search and arrest); United States v. McArthur, 419 F. Supp. 186 (D.N.D. 1975); United States v. Jaramillo, 380 F. Supp. 1375 (D. Neb. 1974).

[88] *See* Hammond, *supra* note 85, at 953, 961, 965–67.

[89] *See Burden*, 288 N.W.2d at 392, *rev'd*, 303 N.W.2d 444; *Taylor*, 645 P.2d at 522.

between the need to call on the military to assist the civilian population during emergencies, and the traditional American reluctance to having the military enforce the civil law. Some scholars argue the Posse Comitatus Act embodies a larger principle of American concern of a standing army that may restrict individual liberties, but the failure to prosecute violations also hints at a desire to continue to have access to the military when dire circumstances arise.[90] Put another way, a court is willing to acknowledge when the military acts beyond its legal mandate, but may find it extremely difficult to convict an Army officer for using his soldiers in a time of crisis to assist civilian authorities.

The Posse Comitatus Act highlights a clear struggle in the American psyche between what Americans want the law to say and what Americans want the military to do in times of crisis. There is an equally compelling struggle right now over the Fourth Amendment's restrictions on police conduct and the application of the exclusionary rule.

III. DEVELOPMENT OF THE EXCLUSIONARY RULE

At the same time the Founding Fathers crafted restrictions on the use of the military inside the United States, they also created protections for citizens from overreaching law enforcement activity.[91] The military restrictions were incorporated into the Constitution, and additional restrictions were added in the Second and Third Amendments to the Constitution.[92] The restrictions on law enforcement were passed with even greater prominence, being both incorporated in the body of the

---

[90] *Cf.* Felicetti & Luce, *supra* note 4, at 91 (arguing that there is "a broader policy or 'spirit' behind the [Posse Comitatus] Act").

[91] *See, e.g.*, U.S. CONST. art. III; *id.* amends. IV, V, VI, VIII.

[92] *See, e.g.*, U.S. CONST. art. I, § 8 (giving Congress appropriations powers over the military, the power to raise a standing army and the power to declare war); *id.* art. II, § 2 (making the military subordinate to the civilian authority of the President); *id.* amend. II (creating the right to a militia under state control and the right of citizens to keep arms); *id.* amend. III (prohibiting the federal government from housing troops in citizens' homes without the consent of the owner); *see also* Laird v. Tatum, 408 U.S. 1, 22–23 (discussing these constitutional rights). There are other restrictions as well, but these are provided as illustration of some key restrictions.

Constitution and added into the Fourth, Fifth, Six, and Eighth Amendments.[93] Similar to the military restrictions mentioned in the previous section, these restrictions were included to address specific abuses by the British government against the Colonies.[94] These blanket restrictions and prohibitions on government conduct created clear individual rights but, with one notable exception, they failed to establish the appropriate remedy, should the government or its agents violate those rights.[95] Over the course of American jurisprudence, courts formulated a doctrine of exclusion, that evidence obtained in violation of constitutional rights should be excluded from the government's efforts to prosecute citizens.[96] This judicial doctrine of excluding evidence obtained by the government in violation of the law was created with the Fourth Amendment.[97]

A. Creation and Growth of the Exclusionary Rule

The Fourth Amendment protects citizens from unreasonable government searches and seizures, but it does not explain what remedies are available for a violation of this constitutional right.[98] The Fourth Amendment to the Constitution reads:

---

[93] *See, e.g.*, U.S. CONST. art. III (creating an independent judiciary and giving Congress the ability to create inferior courts that can examine police conduct); *id.* amend. IV (requiring law enforcement to obtain search warrants and refrain from unreasonable searches); *id.* amend. V (creating a litany of essential rights like due process, the privilege against self-incrimination, the right to indictment by a grand jury and others); *id.* amend. VI (granting the right to speedy trial, right to a jury, right to confrontation of witnesses and right to assistance of counsel); *id.* amend. VIII (prohibiting cruel and unusual punishment, and excessive bail).

[94] 1 HOMER C. HOCKETT, THE CONSTITUTIONAL HISTORY OF THE UNITED STATES, 1776–1826, at 74 (1939); JACOB LANDYNSKI, SEARCH AND SEIZURE AND THE SUPREME COURT: A STUDY IN CONSTITUTIONAL INTERPRETATION 19 (1966).

[95] U.S. CONST. amend. V (providing a remedy by prohibiting self-incrimination).

[96] *See generally* David Gray, *A Spectacular Non Sequitur: The Supreme Court's Contemporary Fourth Amendment Exclusionary Rule Jurisprudence*, 50 AM. CRIM. L. REV. 1 (2013).

[97] *See* U.S. CONST. amend. V; Gray, *supra* note 96; Christine M. D'Elia, Comment, *The Exclusionary Rule: Who Does It Punish?*, 5 SETON HALL CONST. L.J. 563, 564–65 (1995).

[98] *See* U.S. CONST. amend. IV (prohibiting unreasonable searches and seizures and requiring search warrants without proscribing a remedy for violations of these rights).

The right of the people to be secure in their persons, houses, papers, and effects, against unreasonable searches and seizures, shall not be violated, and no Warrants shall issue, but upon probable cause, supported by Oath or affirmation, and particularly describing the place to be searched, and the persons or things to be seized.[99]

Nowhere in the language of this text is a suggestion that the remedy for a violation of the Fourth Amendment is the exclusion of evidence.[100] For almost a century, the courts did not craft any remedy for Fourth Amendment violations.[101] In 1886, the Supreme Court finally addressed the issue of remedies when it created the exclusionary rule in a forfeiture case.[102] In *Boyd v. United States*, the defendant was compelled to produce evidence showing the value and quantity of the goods that were to be forfeited.[103] The goods were ordered forfeited and Boyd appealed, claiming the forced production of evidence was a violation of the Fourth Amendment.[104] The Supreme Court agreed and, for the first time, determined that evidence obtained in violation of the Fourth Amendment should be excluded from court proceedings.[105] This judicial rule of exclusion was created by analogizing to the Fifth Amendment's prohibition of the introduction of compelled testimony.[106] Later courts have disagreed over whether the exclusionary rule is a protection required by the Constitution, or merely a matter of judicial interpretation, or part of the court's "supervisory power."[107] Some courts argue that the exclusionary rule is "not a com-

---

[99] *Id.*
[100] *Id.*; *see also* D'Elia, *supra* note 97, at 563.
[101] *See* Boyd v. United States, 116 U.S. 616 (1886) (excluding evidence obtained in violation of the Fourth Amendment).
[102] *Id.* at 638; *see also* Richard A. Epstein, Entick v Carrington *and* Boyd v United States*: Keeping the Fourth and Fifth Amendments on Track*, 82 U. CHICAGO L. REV. 27 (2015).
[103] *Boyd*, 116 U.S. at 638.
[104] *Id.* at 618.
[105] *Id.* at 638.
[106] U.S. CONST. amend. V (mandating that no person may be compelled "in a criminal case to be a witness against himself"); *Boyd*, 116 U.S. at 633–34.
[107] *See* United States v. Williams, 504 U.S. 36, 50 (1992) (suggesting the exclusionary rule is part of Court's supervisory powers); *see also* WAYNE R. LAFAVE, SEARCH AND SEIZURE: A TREATISE ON THE FOURTH AMENDMENT, § 1.1(d) (5th ed. 2015).

mand of the Fourth Amendment but is a judicially created rule of evidence which Congress may negate."[108] Others disagree, stating that when read in conjunction with the Fifth Amendment, "a constitutional basis emerges which not only justifies but actually requires the exclusionary rule."[109]

This "exclusionary rule" was methodically expanded to encompass more and more Fourth Amendment violations.[110] In *Weeks v. United States*, the Supreme Court excluded evidence seized from an illegal search of the defendant's home.[111] In *Mapp v. Ohio*, the Supreme Court applied the exclusionary rule to state courts for state searches that violated the Fourth Amendment.[112] These cases and others created the foundation of the exclusionary rule, but they only hinted at the overall purpose of excluding competent evidence obtained in violation of the Fourth Amendment.[113]

As courts began to expand the exclusionary rule, they also began to question when it is appropriate to exclude competent evidence of guilt because of inappropriate actions of government officials. Courts have struggled with the fundamental question of whether the exclusionary rule is required by the Constitution, whether it is appropriate for statutory or regulatory violations, and whether a court must determine that excluding evidence satisfies the fundamental purpose of the exclusionary rule.

B. Identifying the Purpose of the Exclusionary Rule

Many judicial opinions exclude evidence when the courts can connect the exclusion to the purpose of the exclusionary rule. A major purpose

---

[108] Wolf v. Colorado, 338 U.S. 25, 28, 32–33 (1949).
[109] Mapp v. Ohio, 367 U.S. 643, 662 (1961) (Black, J., concurring); *see also* TRACEY MACLIN, THE SUPREME COURT AND THE FOURTH AMENDMENT'S EXCLUSIONARY RULE, 88–110, 121–124 (2013).
[110] *See* Weeks v. United States, 232 U.S. 383 (1914) (applying the exclusionary rule to evidence seized from an illegal search); *Wolf*, 338 U.S. at 25.
[111] *Mapp*, 367 U.S. at 662; *see also* MACLIN, *supra* note 109, at 8–14, 17–24.
[112] *Mapp*, 367 U.S. at 656–57.
[113] LAFAVE, *supra* note 107, at § 1.1(f) (stating that *Weeks* and *Boyd* suggest that deterrence is the purpose of the exclusionary rule).

of the exclusionary rule throughout its history has been to deter law enforcement from engaging in unlawful behavior.[114] The exclusionary rule has been justified by its "deterrent safeguard,"[115] that its "purpose is to deter,"[116] and that it is an "effective deterrent to police action."[117] The Supreme Court has emphasized that the "major thrust" of the exclusionary rule is deterrence, but courts have also noted additional purposes for the rule that may justify excluding evidence.[118] Nevertheless, the Supreme Court has justified excluding evidence for purposes other than deterrence as well.

The Supreme Court has stated other purposes for the exclusionary rule. One Supreme Court case noted that the "imperative of judicial integrity" requires courts to exclude evidence obtained in an unconstitutional manner.[119] Another possible purpose is to restore or maintain trust in the government, by ensuring the government does not profit from its unlawful behavior.[120] Another purpose could be to apply the exclusionary rule only where there have been massive institutional failures, at times when law enforcement has pervasive and widespread practice of violating basic constitutional protections.[121]

---

[114] Elkins v. United States, 364 U.S. 206, 210–20 (1960); Terry v. Ohio, 392 U.S. 1, 12 (1968); see also LAFAVE, supra note 107, at § 1.1(f).

[115] Mapp, 367 U.S. at 648–51.

[116] Elkins, 364 U.S. at 217.

[117] Linkletter v. Walker, 381 U.S. 618, 636–37 (1965).

[118] Terry, 392 U.S. at 12–15; see also LAFAVE supra note 111, at 1.1(f).

[119] Elkins, 364 U.S. at 206; see also Robert M. Bloom & David H. Fentin, "A More Majestic Conception": The Importance of Judicial Integrity in Preserving the Exclusionary Rule, 13 U. PA. J. CONST. L. 47, 48 (2010) ("judicial integrity" is the primary purpose of exclusionary rule); Michael D. Cicchini, An Economics Perspective on the Exclusionary Rule and Deterrence, 75 MO. L. REV. 459, 461 (2010) (asserting that the exclusionary rule serves the integrity of the judiciary); Andrew E. Taslitz, Hypocrisy, Corruption, and Illegitimacy: Why Judicial Integrity Justifies the Exclusionary Rule, 10 OHIO ST. J. CRIM. L. 419, 474 (2013) (stating that the exclusionary rule serves judicial integrity).

[120] See United States v. Calandra, 414 U.S. 338, 357 (1974) (Brennan, J., dissenting); Scott E. Sundby, Everyman's Exclusionary Rule: The Exclusionary Rule and the Rule of Law (or Why Conservatives Should Embrace the Exclusionary Rule), 10 OHIO ST. J. CRIM. L. 393, 397–98 (2013) (arguing that the rule of law and the ordinary citizen's belief in it is a justification for the exclusionary rule). This concept rests on the idea that the trust of citizens in the U.S. government will be increased when the citizens know the government cannot benefit from unconstitutional activity. Id.

[121] See John Kaplan, The Limits of the Exclusionary Rule, 26 STAN. L. REV. 1027, 1050 (1974).

Academics have argued for other justifications for the exclusionary rule.[122] Understanding the purpose of the exclusionary rule is essential to determining when the court should suppress evidence and when it should not.

Although other purposes behind the exclusionary rule have been cited, the Supreme Court has for decades focused on the primary purpose of deterring future police misconduct as the basis for suppressing evidence.[123] In recent years, the Supreme Court has emphasized the deterrence purpose of the exclusionary rule over all other possible purposes.[124] In *Herring v. United States*, the majority and dissenting opinions demonstrate a stark contrast in the debate over the purpose of the exclusionary rule, and the effect it has on the application of the exclusionary rule to the facts of each case.[125] The defendant was arrested and his truck was searched based on inaccurate information from the police department of a different county.[126] During the search, and based on the mistaken belief that there was a warrant, the officers found a firearm and methamphetamine.[127] The defendant was charged with drug and firearm offenses, and he moved to suppress the evidence against him.[128] The parties before the Supreme Court agreed that the search was unlawful, but the government argued that the exclusionary rule should not apply because the mistake was the result of a bookkeeping error, and therefore suppression would have no deterrent effect.[129]

---

[122] *See, e.g.,* William A. Schroeder, *Restoring the Status Quo Ante: The Fourth Amendment Exclusionary Rule as a Compensating Device*, 51 GEO. WASH. L. REV. 633, 636 (1983).

[123] *See, e.g.,* INS v. Lopez-Mendoza, 468 U.S. 1032 (1984); United States v. Leon, 468 U.S. 897 (1984); Stone v. Powell, 428 U.S. 465 (1976); United States v. Janis, 428 U.S. 433 (1976).

[124] *See* Davis v. United States, 564 U.S. 229, 238 (2011). *See generally* Scott E. Sundby and Lucy B. Ricca, *The Majestic and the Mundane: The Two Creation Stories of the Exclusionary Rule*, 43 TEX. TECH L. REV. 391 (2010).

[125] *See* Herring v. United States, 555 U.S. 135, 141 n.2 (2009) (majority opinion); *id.* at 151–53 (Ginsberg, J., dissenting).

[126] *Id.* at 137–38.

[127] *Id.*

[128] *Id.* at 138.

[129] *Id.* at 137.

The five-justice majority found that deterrence is the "purpose" of the exclusionary rule.[130] The Supreme Court held that the exclusionary rule "forbids the use of improperly obtained evidence at trial."[131] Since the Fourth Amendment violation was a mistake, there was no deterrent effect in suppressing the evidence against Herring.[132] The majority emphasized that the only legitimate purpose of the exclusionary rule is deterrence.[133] If suppressing evidence will not deter future police misconduct, then suppression of improperly obtained evidence is not appropriate.

The dissent argued that the evidence obtained in violation of the Fourth Amendment should be suppressed because of other important purposes behind the exclusionary rule.[134] Although the dissent concurs that the primary purpose of the exclusionary rule is deterrence, the dissent argues that the need to preserve judicial integrity and ensure that the government does not profit from its wrongdoing is also an essential "purpose" of the exclusionary rule.[135] The *Herring* majority disagreed with this concept of multiple purposes for the exclusionary rule, and the Supreme Court began to restrict the reach of the exclusionary rule to only those cases in which it would have a deterrent effect on future police behavior.[136]

In *Davis v. United States*, the Supreme Court affirmed the *Herring* view that that deterrence is the only legitimate purpose of the exclusionary rule, stating:[137]

---

[130] *Id.* at 139-40 (quoting United States v. Calandra, 414 U.S. 338, 348 (1974)).

[131] *Id.* ("We have stated that this judicially created rule is designed to safeguard Fourth Amendment rights generally through its deterrent effect.")

[132] *Id.* at 140 (connecting the officers' mistaken belief that a warrant existed to the Fourth Amendment and the court's holding of the deterrence purpose).

[133] *Id.*; *see also* Sundby & Ricca, *supra* note 124, at 392–93 (asserting prime intention of exclusionary rule through analysis of landmark exclusionary cases).

[134] *See Herring*, 555 U.S. at 151–52 (Ginsburg, J., dissenting) (quoting Justice Stevens's dissent in Arizona v. Evans, 514 U.S. 1, 18 (1995)).

[135] *See id.* (quoting Potter Stewart, *The Road to Mapp v. Ohio and Beyond: The Origins, Development and Future of the Exclusionary Rule in Search-and-Seizure Cases*, 83 COLUM. L. Rev. 1365, 1389 (1983)).

[136] *See id.*

[137] *See* Davis v. United States, 564 U.S. 229, 236 (2011).

[i]t is one thing for the criminal "to go free because the constable has blundered." It is quite another to set the criminal free because the constable has scrupulously adhered to governing law. Excluding evidence in such cases deters no police misconduct and imposes substantial social costs.[138]

The Court explained that "real deterrent value is a 'necessary condition for exclusion,'" and excluding evidence is inappropriate if it would not deter future police conduct.[139] The majority rejected the idea that there were other legitimate purposes to suppress evidence.[140]

The *Davis* Court also emphasized that the exclusionary rule is not required by the Constitution, but is "is a 'prudential' doctrine, created by this Court to 'compel respect for the constitutional guaranty.'"[141] As a judicially created rule, the Court stressed it must be narrowly applied only when necessary to satisfy its sole purpose of deterrence.[142]

The dissent in *Davis* vigorously criticized the majority opinion.[143] While the dissent argued about retroactivity and the applicability of new constitutional rules to pending cases, its main disagreement with the majority concerned the "purpose" of the exclusionary rule.[144] The dissent argued that the majority opinion "will undermine the exclusionary rule" and limit its reach to only those cases where it will deter future police misconduct.[145]

This recent emphasis on the application of the exclusionary rule to only Fourth Amendment violations that will deter future police conduct is a significant reduction in the application and effect of the exclusionary rule. Prior to this restriction, the exclusionary rule was

---

[138] *Id.* at 249 (quoting People v. Defore, 242 N.Y. 13, 21, 150 N.E. 585, 587 (1926) (Cardozo, J.)).
[139] *Id.* at 237 (quoting Hudson v. Michigan, 547 U.S. 586, 596 (2006)).
[140] *Id.*
[141] *See id.* at 236 (explaining that the text of the Fourth Amendment lacks reference to the suppression of any evidence obtained through its violation) (quoting Pennsylvania Bd. of Probation and Parole v. Scott, 524 U.S. 357, 363 (1998), and Elkins v. United States, 364 U.S. 206, 217 (1960)).
[142] *Id.* at 236–37 (citing United States v. Calandra, 414 U.S. 338, 348 (1965)).
[143] *See id.* at 252 (Breyer, J., dissenting).
[144] *See id.* at 256–57.
[145] *See id.* at 257–60.

applied to non-constitutional violations of law.[146] This renewed focus on excluding evidence that was derived from only constitutional violations will impact a significant portion of exclusionary-rule jurisprudence.

C. Applying the Exclusionary Rule Beyond Fourth Amendment Violations

The Supreme Court has now emphasized the specific purpose of the exclusionary rule is to deter future police misconduct by suppressing evidence obtained in unconstitutional searches and seizures, which is a departure from past case law.[147] Historically, the exclusionary rule was used in cases that did not involve constitutional violations.[148] In those cases, courts suppressed evidence obtained by the government in violation of statutes, regulations, and other non-constitutional violations.[149] The recent Supreme Court jurisprudence in *Herring* and *Davis* has significantly limited the exclusionary rule's application in non-constitutional violations of law.[150] This new line of cases limiting the application of the exclusionary rule conflicts with the cases that address Posse Comitatus Act violations.

The Supreme Court and other federal courts have emphasized that violating government regulations is insufficient to trigger the exclusionary rule.[151] In *United States v. Caceres*, the Supreme Court held that suppression of tape recordings was not appropriate when the recordings were obtained in compliance with the Fourth Amendment but in violation of Internal Revenue Service ("IRS") regulations.[152]

---

[146] *See, e.g.*, Sanchez–Llamas v. Oregon, 548 U.S. 331, 348 (2006); Miller v. United States, 357 U.S. 301, 313–14 (1958); McNabb v. United States, 318 U.S. 332, 344–45, (1943) (stating that the exclusionary rule requires notice and is used to avoid illegal interrogations that lead to unreliable confessions).
[147] Herring v. United States, 555 U.S. 135, 141 (2009).
[148] *See* United States v. Caceres, 440 U.S. 741, 749–50 (1979).
[149] *See* Anthony G. Amsterdam, *Perspectives on the Fourth Amendment*, 58 MINN. L. REV. 349, 416–428 (1974). *See generally* Carl McGowan, *Rule-Making and the Police*, 70 MICH. L. REV. 659 (1972).
[150] *Davis*, 564 U.S. at 236–38.
[151] *Caceres*, 440 U.S. at 754–56; *see also* Recent Case, United States v. Dreyer, 767 F.3d 826 (9th Cir. 2014), 128 HARV. L. REV. 1876, 1880–81 (2015).
[152] *Caceres*, 440 U.S. at 756–57.

Caceres was decided three decades before the Supreme Court started limiting the application and purpose of the exclusionary rule.[153] In *Caceres*, the Court rejected the application of the exclusionary rule to agency regulations, noting that "rigid application of an exclusionary rule to every regulatory violation could have a serious deterrent impact on the formulation of additional standards to govern prosecutorial and police procedures."[154] While the Supreme Court stopped short of declaring that exclusion of evidence is never appropriate for non-constitutional regulatory violations, circuit courts of appeals have more forcefully argued the inapplicability of the exclusionary rule to regulatory violations.[155]

In *Sanchez-Llamas v. Oregon*, the Supreme Court determined that the exclusionary rule should not be applied to violations of the right to consular notifications under a treaty.[156] The Court explained that the exclusionary rule should be used primarily "to deter constitutional violations" and only used to suppress evidence for statutory violations in rare cases where "the evidence arose out of statutory violations that implicated important Fourth and Fifth Amendment interests."[157] The Court reaffirmed that the focus of the exclusionary rule was to deter constitutional violations.

Circuit courts of appeals have followed the Supreme Court's reluctance to apply the exclusionary rule to statutory and regulatory violations.[158] In *United States v. Lomberga-Camorlinga*, the Ninth Circuit Court of Appeals determined that the exclusionary rule should not be used to suppress evidence in violation of a treaty.[159] The treaty required law enforcement officers to notify a foreign national that he

---

[153] *Id.* at 741; Herring v. United States, 555 U.S. 135 (2009).
[154] *Caceres*, 440 U.S. at 755–56.
[155] *See* United States v. Hinton, 222 F.3d 664, 674 (9th Cir. 2000); United States v. Lombera-Camorlinga, 206 F.3d 882, 886 (9th Cir. 2000) (*en banc*).
[156] Sanchez-Llamas v. Oregon, 548 U.S. 331, 348 (2006).
[157] *Id.* at 348; *see also Caceres*, 440 U.S. at 754–57.
[158] *See Lombera-Camorlinga*, 206 F.3d at 886; United States v. Adams, 740 F.3d 40, 43–44 (1st Cir. 2014); United States v. Abdi, 463 F.3d 547. 556–57 (6th Cir. 2006).
[159] *Lombera-Camorlinga*, 206 F.3d at 886.

has a right to notify his consulate that he was arrested.[160] Citing numerous other circuits, the Ninth Circuit *en banc* panel determined that the "exclusionary rule is typically available only for constitutional violations, not for statutory or treaty violations."[161]

In *United States v. Adams*, the First Circuit concurred, finding that the exclusionary rule should not apply to government violations of statutes.[162] The First Circuit found that "statutory violations, untethered to the abridgment of constitutional rights, are not sufficiently egregious to justify suppression."[163] The Sixth Circuit agreed, stating in *United States v. Abdi*, "the exclusionary rule is an appropriate sanction for a statutory violation only where the statute specifically provides for suppression as a remedy or the statutory violation implicates underlying constitutional rights such as the right to be free from unreasonable search and seizure."[164] These courts have emphasized that Congress alone should write the exclusionary rule into a statute, and courts should not read into a statutory scheme an exclusionary remedy when Congress has prescribed a remedy other than exclusion.[165] These circuit courts stress that the exclusionary rule should be

---

[160] *Id.*; Vienna Convention on Consular Relations art. 36, April 24, 1963, 21 U.S.T. 77, 596 U.N.T.S. 261.

[161] *Lombera-Camorlinga*, 206 F.3d at 886; *see also* United States v. Smith, 196 F.3d 1034, 1040 (9th Cir. 1999) ("The use of the exclusionary rule is an exceptional remedy typically reserved for violations of constitutional rights."); United States v. Ware, 161 F.3d 414, 424 (6th Cir. 1998) (holding a statutory violation insufficient to justify imposition of the exclusionary rule, absent an underlying constitutional violation or right); United States v. Mason, 52 F.3d 1286, 1289 n.5 (4th Cir. 1995); United States v. Thompson, 936 F.2d 1249, 1251 (11th Cir. 1991) (holding a statutory violation insufficient to justify imposition of the exclusionary rule, absent an underlying constitutional violation or right or evidence that Congress intended exclusion as a remedy); United States v. Benevento, 836 F.2d 60, 69 (2d Cir. 1987); United States v. Kington, 801 F.2d 733, 737 (5th Cir. 1986); United States v. Hensel, 699 F.2d 18, 29 (1st Cir. 1983) (rejecting suppression as a remedy for a treaty violation because the exclusionary rule "was not fashioned to vindicate a broad, general right to be free of agency action not 'authorized' by law, but rather to protect certain specific, constitutionally protected rights of individuals.").

[162] *Adams*, 740 F.3d at 43–44.

[163] *Id.*

[164] United States v. Abdi, 463 F.3d 547, 556–57 (6th Cir. 2006).

[165] *See, e.g.*, United States v. Forrester, 512 F.3d 500, 512–13 (9th Cir. 2008) (pen register statute); United States v. Feng, 277 F.3d 1151, 1154 (9th Cir. 2002) (prosecutor's alleged

limited to constitutional violations, and only be used for statutory violations when authorized by Congress, or when the statute is so closely connected to a constitutional right that the exclusionary rule is needed to protect that right.

Suppression of evidence is also not appropriate for a violation of agency regulations.[166] In *United States v. Hinton*, the Ninth Circuit Court of Appeals categorically stated, "suppression is not the appropriate remedy for a failure to follow agency regulations."[167] *Hinton*—another case decided prior to *Herring* and *Davis*—stressed that the exclusionary rule was designed to apply to constitutional violations, not regulatory ones.[168] The court clearly stated that the "relevant inquiry is whether a constitutional right, not an agency regulation, has been violated."[169] *Hinton* and other circuit cases are entirely consistent with the shift in the Supreme Court's view of the purpose of the exclusionary rule.[170]

The Supreme Court has also confirmed that the exclusionary rule should only be applied when it deters police misconduct.[171] The Court and subsequent Ninth Circuit cases emphasize that the exclusionary rule should only apply to conduct that violates the Constitution, not to lesser violations of statutes or agency regulations.[172] Despite this long line of cases restricting the use of the exclusionary rule, courts have considered applying it to the violation of the Posse Comitatus Act, a statute, and to agency regulations that apply the statutory proscriptions. These views on the purpose of the exclusionary rule are at odds with the evolving views on the role of the military in domestic law enforcement. Courts still consider applying the exclusionary rule

---

violation of criminal bribery statute); United States v. Michaelian, 803 F.2d 1042, 1049 (9th Cir. 1986) (unauthorized IRS disclosure of tax return information).
[166] *See* United States v. Hinton, 222 F.3d 664, 674 (9th Cir. 2000).
[167] *Id.*
[168] *Id.* at 675.
[169] *Id.*
[170] *Id.*; *see also* United States v. Ani, 138 F.3d 390, 392 (9th Cir. 1998) (holding the exclusionary rule was not applicable to a non-constitutional violation of U.S. Customs regulation).
[171] Herring v. United States, 555 U.S. 135, 141–43 (2009).
[172] United States v. Caceres, 440 U.S. 741, 755–56 (1979); *Hinton*, 222 F.3d at 674–75.

to a criminal statute, and regulations implementing it, when the acts concern the use of the military as law enforcement.

IV. THE EXCLUSIONARY RULE AND THE POSSE COMITATUS ACT

The Ninth Circuit's application of the exclusionary rule to the Posse Comitatus Act is inconsistent with evolving Supreme Court doctrine. The Posse Comitatus Act is a criminal statute; the violation of it carries a fine and prison for the actor.[173] In 1878, Congress did not write in the act that evidence derived in violation of the Posse Comitatus Act should be excluded in a criminal trial, and it has not added one in the 140 years since its enactment.[174] The Posse Comitatus Act applies to the Navy and Marine Corps not by its language, but indirectly, through congressionally mandated agency regulations.[175] The exclusionary rule should not apply to Posse Comitatus Act violations because a violation of the act is not a constitutional violation. Although some courts have been reluctant to apply an exclusionary rule to Posse Comitatus Act cases in the past, other courts have freely applied it to evidence seized during a Posse Comitatus Act violation.

The current Supreme Court guidance is that the exclusionary rule should only be used to suppress evidence derived from constitutional violations, and only be used when it will likely deter future police misconduct. Application of the exclusionary rule to Posse Comitatus Act violations does not fit well into either purpose. This section will explore the cases that have struggled to find the appropriate connection between the improper use of the military to assist in law enforcement activities and the evidence obtained from that improper use.

---

[173] Posse Comitatus Act, §15, 20 Stat. 152 (1878) (codified as amended at 18 U.S.C. § 1385 (2016)).

[174] *Id.* Congress amended the statute only once, to include the Air Force after it was separated from the Army pursuant to the National Security Act of 1947.

[175] *See* 10 U.S.C. § 275 (2016) (renumbered from section 375); DEP'T OF DEFENSE, DOD INSTRUCTION 3025.21, DEFENSE SUPPORT OF CIVILIAN LAW ENFORCEMENT AGENCIES (Feb. 27, 2013).

A. The Posse Comitatus Act and Wounded Knee

The Posse Comitatus Act was a little-used and relatively obscure statute for almost a century, until it became prominent in the criminal cases that resulted from an incident at Wounded Knee, South Dakota, in 1973.[176] A group protesting the treatment of Native Americans took control of the small town of Wounded Knee.[177] State and federal law enforcement officers responded and issued orders prohibiting individuals from bypassing law enforcement roadblocks and entering the town.[178] The military also responded to provide assistance to law enforcement.[179] Several individuals were arrested and prosecuted for crimes including obstructing a law enforcement officer in the lawful performance of his duties during the course of a civil disturbance.[180] Four defendants, charged in separate cases raised a claim that the military involvement with civilian law enforcement required an acquittal.[181] The defendants claimed that their convictions should be overturned because the military's assistance to law enforcement violated the Posse Comitatus Act.[182] The defendants argued that an essential element of the charged crime required that the law enforcement officers were lawfully engaged in their duties.[183] Since law enforcement called on the military in violation of federal law, the

---

[176] United States v. McArthur, 419 F. Supp. 186 (D.N.D. 1975); United States v. Red Feather, 392 F. Supp. 916 (D.S.D. 1975); United States v. Banks, 383 F. Supp. 389 (D.S.D. 1974); United States v. Jaramillo, 380 F. Supp. 1375 (D. Neb. 1974).

[177] *Cf. Jaramillo*, 380 F. Supp. at 1376.

[178] Andrew H. Malcolm, *Occupation of Wounded Knee is Ended*, N.Y. TIMES (May 8, 1973), https://archive.nytimes.com/www.nytimes.com/learning/general/onthisday/big/0508.html.

[179] *Red Feather*, 392 F.Supp. at 921.

[180] 18 U.S.C. § 231(a)(3) (1970), *amended by* 18 U.S.C. § 231(1994). *See Jaramillo*, 380 F. Supp. 1375; *Banks*, 383 F. Supp. 368; *Red Feather*, 392 F. Supp. 916; *McArthur*, 419 F. Supp. 186.

[181] *Jaramillo*, 380 F. Supp. 1375; *Banks*, 383 F. Supp. 368; *Red Feather*, 392 F. Supp. 916; *McArthur*, 419 F. Supp. 186.

[182] *See Jaramillo*, 380 F. Supp. 1375; *Banks*, 383 F. Supp. 368; *Red Feather*, 392 F. Supp. 916; *McArthur*, 419 F. Supp. 186.

[183] 18 U.S.C. § 231(a)(3) (whoever obstructs a "law enforcement officer lawfully engaged in the lawful performance of his official duties . . .").

defendants claimed, the military was not engaged in lawful duties and the convictions should not stand.[184]

Separate courts reached different conclusions on whether the military's actions violated the Posse Comitatus Act.[185] These cases did not specifically discuss the exclusionary rule. Rather, the issue was whether the government could prove an essential element of the crime if the military violated the Posse Comitatus Act.[186] However, the Wounded Knee cases provided different and conflicting ways to evaluate whether the military acted in violation of the Posse Comitatus Act, and opened the door for other defendants to argue that suppression of evidence is the appropriate remedy when the military unlawfully engages in law enforcement activity.

B. Suppressing Evidence in Posse Comitatus Act Violations

The Wounded Knee cases challenged the lawfulness of police conduct when the military assists them in law enforcement activities. These cases led to the next logical step: defendants requesting the suppression of evidence gathered by the military in violation of the Posse Comitatus Act.[187] While the Supreme Court has never ruled on a Posse Comitatus case, the lower state and federal courts developed a consistent pattern. These cases arose long before the Supreme Court

---

[184] *Red Feather*, 392 F. Supp. at 925; *see also Jaramillo*, 380 F. Supp. at 1381 (upholding acquittal on charge of obstructing law enforcement officers at Wounded Knee on grounds that the prosecution failed to prove that the Posse Comitatus Act was not violated by the military's contributions to the operation, thus raising a reasonable doubt as to whether the law enforcement officers were lawfully engaged in the performance of duties). *But see McArthur*, 419 F. Supp. at 194 (holding that evidence of military activity at Wounded Knee was insufficient to overcome presumption that law enforcement officers acted in performance of duties).

[185] *See Jaramillo*, 380 F. Supp. at 1381 (holding that the military's actions violated the Posse Comitatus Act); *Banks*, 383 F. Supp. at 376 (stating that the military's actions violated the Posse Comitatus Act); *Red Feather*, 392 F. Supp. at 925 (stating that the military's supporting actions did not violate the Posse Comitatus Act).

[186] *See Jaramillo*, 380 F. Supp. at 1375; *Banks*, 383 F. Supp. at 368; *Red Feather*, 392 F. Supp. at 916.

[187] *See* United States v. Walden, 490 F.2d 372 (4th Cir. 1974); *see also* United States v. Griley, 814 F.2d 967 (4th Cir. 1987).

began narrowing the application of the exclusionary rule to its purpose to deter police misconduct, and the courts developed a common response to requests to suppress evidence obtained by the military in violation of the Posse Comitatus Act.

In the pre-*Herring* cases, courts noted that the Posse Comitatus Act does not contain a provision calling for suppression of evidence obtained in violation of the act.[188] Courts have noted that Congress has the option to write the exclusionary rule into statutes, but chose instead to use criminal sanctions to deter military misconduct.[189] The courts then note that lower courts could create an exclusionary rule for violations of the Posse Comitatus Act, just as the Supreme Court did for Fourth Amendment violations in *Boyd*.[190] Each court then determined whether there existed "widespread and repeated violations" of the Posse Comitatus Act that warranted judicial creation and employment of the exclusionary rule.[191]

In *United States v. Walden*, the Fourth Circuit Court of Appeals noted that there was no statutory exclusionary rule for the Posse Comitatus Act and declined to create one where the defendant alleged that U.S. Marine Corps investigators obtained evidence in violation of the Posse Comitatus Act.[192] The Fourth Circuit reaffirmed this rule in 1995, when the court found that the exclusionary rule is not available

---

[188] *See, e.g., Griley*, 814 F.2d at 976 (holding that the exclusionary rule does not apply to violations of the Posse Comitatus Act, and finding no grounds to apply the exclusionary rule based on the facts of the case).

[189] *See* 18 U.S.C. § 1385 (2016) (criminalizing the use of the Army and Air Force to execute the laws, and providing a two-year maximum sentence for violations).

[190] Boyd v. United States, 116 U.S. 616 (1886); *see also Griley*, 814 F.2d at 976.

[191] *Walden*, 490 F.2d at 372 (acknowledging that the exclusionary rule could apply, but declining to exclude evidence in that case); *see also* United States v. Dreyer, 804 F.3d 1266, 1278–79 (9th Cir. 2015) (*en banc*) (stating exclusionary rule is available but declined to apply it to the facts in that case); *Griley*, 814 F.2d at 976 (stating there is no exclusionary rule for Posse Comitatus Act violations and no reason to adopt one in that case); Taylor v. State, 645 P.2d 522 (Okla. Crim. App. 1982) (excluding evidence derived from a violation of the Posse Comitatus Act).

[192] *Walden*, 490 F.2d at 372; *see also* Griley, 814 F.2d at 967 (stating that there is no exclusionary rule for Posse Comitatus Act violations and no reason to adopt one in that case).

for violations of the Posse Comitatus Act.[193] The *Al-Talib* court emphasized that the exclusionary rule is clearly unavailable when the military did not seize any evidence.[194] The Fifth and Seventh Circuit Courts of Appeals concurred in this view; both noted that the statute lacks an exclusionary rule and both declined to create one when the case before them did not involve widespread and repeated violations.[195]

The Ninth Circuit also agreed.[196] In dealing with allegations that the U.S. Navy violated regulations that impose Posse Comitatus Act-like restrictions, the court determined "an exclusionary rule should not be applied to violations [of regulations that apply the Posse Comitatus Act to the Navy] until a need to deter future violations is demonstrated."[197]

State courts also shared in this view. The Alaska appellate court found there was no exclusionary rule applicable to Posse Comitatus Act violations and no reason to create one without widespread or repeated violations.[198] The Washington State Supreme Court went further to state that there is no exclusionary rule for evidence obtained in violation of the Posse Comitatus Act.[199] Florida and Kansas have also issued similar rulings, noting that there is no exclusionary rule in the Posse Comitatus Act and declining to create a judicially imposed exclusionary rule.[200] Each of the state and federal courts who reviewed potential Posse Comitatus Act violations declined to impose the exclusionary rule and suppress evidence derived from the alleged violations. However, each court noted it could create an exclusionary

---

[193] United States v. Al-Talib, 55 F.3d 923 (1995).

[194] *Id.*

[195] United States v. Wolffs, 594 F.2d 77 (5th Cir. 1979); United States v. Hartley, 796 F.2d 112 (5th Cir. 1986); Hayes v. Hawes, 921 F.2d 100 (7th Cir. 1990).

[196] United States v. Roberts 779 F.2d 565, 568 (9th Cir. 1986).

[197] *Id.* at 568 (citing *Wolffs*, 594 F.2d at 77, 85, and *Walden*, 490 F.2d at 376–77).

[198] Moon v. State, 785 P.2d 45 (Alaska Ct. App. 1990) (the court noted there was no history of Posse Comitatus Act violations in Alaska).

[199] State v. Valdobinos, 858 P.2d 199 (Wash. 1993).

[200] *See* Taylor v. State, 640 So. 2d 1127 (Fla. Dist. Ct. App. 1994) (holding that the exclusionary rule should not be applied, although the Naval Investigative Service's involvement may have violated the Posse Comitatus Act); State v. Roberts, 786 P.2d 630 (Kan. Ct. App. 1990) (finding that even if a violation of the Posse Comitatus Act occurred, the extraordinary remedy of exclusion is not appropriate).

rule if the military engaged in "widespread and repeated violations" of the Posse Comitatus Act or its implementing regulations.[201]

All of these cases preceded the Supreme Court's recent exclusionary-rule restrictions.[202] Although these cases noted the possibility of creating an exclusionary rule for Posse Comitatus Act violations, each court declined to suppress evidence in situations where the Posse Comitatus Act was violated.[203] Since courts were reluctant to apply the exclusionary rule even before the Supreme Court's recent declaration that the exclusionary rule should only be used for constitutional violations, and only when it will deter future police misconduct, it seemed likely that the exclusionary rule would never be applied to the Posse Comitatus Act. Yet in *United States v. Dreyer*, the Ninth Circuit took a different path.

C. The *Dreyer* Decision

The Ninth Circuit was the first appellate court to revisit the application of the exclusionary rule to the Posse Comitatus Act after the Supreme Court decisions in *Herring* and *Davis*.[204] In *Dreyer*, a Navy Criminal Investigative Service ("NCIS") agent used a software program to search for child pornography on the internet.[205] The NCIS agent conducted a broad search of all computers in the state of Washington, not just the computers of those in the military.[206] The

---

[201] *See supra* notes 199, 200; *infra* note and 202.

[202] *See* Hudson v. Michigan, 547 U.S. 586, 591 (2006) (finding that the exclusionary rule is applicable "where its remedial objectives are thought most efficaciously served" (quoting United States v. Calandra, 414 U.S. 338, 348 (1974)).

[203] *See* United States v. Dreyer, 804 F.3d 1266, 1279 (9th Cir. 2015) (*en banc*); United States v. Griley, 814 F.2d 967 (4th Cir. 1987) (holding that the exclusionary rule does not apply to violations of the Posse Comitatus Act, and finding no grounds to apply the exclusionary rule based on the facts of the case); State v. Roberts, 786 F.2d 630 (Kan. Ct. App. 1990); *Taylor*, 640 So. 2d 1127.

[204] *Dreyer*, 767 F.3d 826 (9th Cir. 2014), *rev'd*, 804 F.3d 1266.

[205] *Dreyer*, 767 F.3d at 827, 830–31 (holding that although the agent was a civilian, the Posse Comitatus Act restrictions applied to civilian officers working for the Navy (citing United States v. Chon, 210 F.3d 990, 993 (9th Cir. 2000))).

[206] *Id.* at 827.

software was only able to access information that was publicly available, so the search complied with the Fourth Amendment.[207]

The NCIS agent found evidence of child pornography, determined it belonged to someone outside of the military, and turned it over to local law enforcement.[208] The local officer obtained a search warrant for the computer, found the child pornography, and Dreyer was charged in federal court.[209] Dreyer moved to suppress the evidence of child pornography, claiming that the search conducted by the NCIS agent violated the Posse Comitatus Act and that the exclusionary rule should apply.[210] The district court denied the motion, Dreyer was convicted at trial, and he appealed both his conviction and the denial of the motion to suppress.[211]

The three-judge appellate panel found that the NCIS agent did violate the regulations implementing the Posse Comitatus Act when he conducted an internet search in the state of Washington for evidence of child pornography.[212] The court then turned to the question of whether the exclusionary rule should apply to suppress the evidence gathered in violation of the Posse Comitatus Act.[213] The panel held that the evidence gathered in violation of the Posse Comitatus Act should be suppressed.[214]

The three-judge panel ignored the recent Supreme Court cases that restricted the use of a judicially created exclusionary rule and instead focused on an old Ninth Circuit precedent that contemplated creating an exclusionary rule for the Posse Comitatus Act if there were "widespread and repeated violations."[215] The court emphasized that Posse Comitatus Act violations of the NCIS agent were "widespread and repeated," therefore they believed that the evidence should be excluded. The government appealed this decision and the Ninth Circuit granted rehearing *en banc*.

---

[207] *See id.*
[208] *Id.* at 828.
[209] *Id.* at 828–29.
[210] *Id.* at 829.
[211] *Id.*
[212] *Id.* at 832.
[213] *Id.* at 835–36.
[214] *Id.* at 837.
[215] *Id.* at 836 (citing United States v. Roberts, 779 F.2d 565, 568 (9th Cir. 1986)).

The *en banc* court affirmed the determination that the NCIS violated the Posse Comitatus Act, but declined to suppress the evidence.[216] However, the Ninth Circuit decision significantly departs from Supreme Court precedent. The Ninth Circuit found that the exclusionary rule was available, but declined to apply it to the facts in this case.[217] In doing so, the court misinterpreted Supreme Court precedent and inverted the test to determine when the exclusionary rule should apply.[218]

The *Dreyer* court misinterprets Supreme Court precedent. *Dreyer* acknowledged that the Supreme Court in *Hudson v. Michigan* began to restrict the scope of the exclusionary rule.[219] But the *en banc* court dismissed the cases that limited the exclusionary rule solely to violations of constitutional rights.[220] The Ninth Circuit argued that the Supreme Court sanctions the use of the exclusionary rule to enforce some statutes, although each case it cited as support were actually fifty-year-old cases that had Fourth and Fifth Amendment violations.[221] The court never cited *Herring* and mentioned *Davis* only in passing.[222] Once the Ninth Circuit had softened Supreme Court precedent to establish that the exclusionary rule may be applicable for statutory violations, the court then turned to the issue of whether the exclusionary rule could be applied to Posse Comitatus Act violations.[223] The court determined it could because the Supreme Court had never specifically ruled that the exclusionary rule did not apply to *this* statute, stating, "We know of no controlling precedent precluding application of the exclusionary rule for a violation of the [Posse Comitatus Act or the regulations that apply it to the Navy]."[224] The Ninth Circuit ignored *Sanchez-Llamas*, which stated that the exclusionary rule

---

[216] *Dreyer*, 804 F.3d 1266, 1279 (9th Cir. 2015) (*en banc*).
[217] *Id.* at 1279–80.
[218] *Id.* at 1278–79.
[219] *Dreyer*, 767 F.3d at 839 (O'Scannlain, J., concurring in part and dissenting in part) (citing Hudson v. Michigan, 547 U.S. 586, 591 (2006)).
[220] *Dreyer*, 804 F.3d at 1278–79.
[221] *Id.* at 1278–79.
[222] *Id.* at 1278.
[223] *Id.* at 1279.
[224] *Id.*

should not be used for non-constitutional violations of statutes.[225] The Ninth Circuit stated the Posse Comitatus Act has "constitutional underpinnings," citing the Third Amendment and legislative history.[226] After diminishing Supreme Court precedent to allow exclusion of evidence for statutory violation not specifically precluded by a Supreme Court opinion, it ultimately declined to apply the exclusionary rule, but strongly stated that it would if there were future violations by the military.[227] Therefore, the highest court to address this issue, and its most recent decision, holds that the exclusionary rule is an available remedy for violations of the Posse Comitatus Act.

V. RECONCILING THE POSSE COMITATUS ACT AND THE EXCLUSIONARY RULE

The *Dreyer* decision conflicts with the recent line of Supreme Court cases on the application of the exclusionary rule. The decision in *Dreyer* is incorrect, but understandable. The Ninth Circuit was reacting to the same concerns that led to the passage of the Posse Comitatus Act one and a half centuries ago. The military engaged in law enforcement activity, and did so at the direction at the local and low-level civil officials. The facts demonstrated the military engaged in law enforcement without regard for the traditional restrictions placed on the military when enforcing the law. While the actions of the Navy investigators were improper, using the exclusionary rule to suppress evidence is contrary to Supreme Court precedent. The exclusionary rule should not be used for government misconduct that violates a statute or a regulation. Further, the exclusionary rule should only be used to deter *police* misconduct. These two issues will be explored below.

---

[225] Sanchez-Llamas v. Oregon, 548 U.S. 331, 348 (2006); *see also* United States v. Caceres, 440 U.S. 741, 754–57 (1979).
[226] *Dreyer*, 804 F.3d at 1279.
[227] *Id.* at 1279–80.

A. The Exclusionary Rule and Violation of Statutes

The exclusionary rule is an extraordinary remedy, one that should be used as a "last resort."[228] It should not be used for a violation of a statute.[229] There is a simple reason for this: Congress declined to write the exclusionary rule into the statute they created. Congress created the statutory rules that govern police and military behavior when it enacted the Posse Comitatus Act. Congress also determined the consequences for violating its rules—offenders could be fined and imprisoned for violating the act. Congress chose to use criminal sanctions to punish persons for using the military as law enforcement. The Supreme Court in *Herring* and *Davis* held that courts should use the exclusionary rule for constitutional violations, not statutory violations.[230]

Congress could have written an exclusionary rule into the Posse Comitatus Act, and Congress could also have added an exclusionary rule to the act in the 140 years since it became law. Congress wrote exclusionary rules into other statutes in the last 140 years.[231] Since Congress has not chosen to specifically exclude any evidence derived from the use of the military to enforce the laws, the courts should not presume that Congress wants exclusion of evidence as a remedy. Evidence derived from a violation of the Posse Comitatus Act should be admissible in a criminal trial.

B. The Exclusionary Rule and Deterring Police Misconduct

Excluding evidence resulting from the misuse of the military in civilian law enforcement does not deter future police misconduct.

---

[228] Hudson v. Michigan, 547 U.S. 586, 589 (2006).
[229] *See Sanchez-Llamas*, 548 U.S. at 34–49.
[230] *See e.g.*, Davis v. United States, 564 U.S. 229, 236–37 (2011) (primary purpose of exclusionary rule is to deter Fourth Amendment violations); Herring v. United States, 555 U.S. 135, 141 (2009) (primary purpose of exclusionary rule is to deter Fourth Amendment violations).
[231] *See, e.g.*, 18 U.S.C. § 2518(10)(a) (2016); Foreign Intelligence Surveillance Act, 50 U.S.C. §§ 1806, 1825, 1845 (2016).

Violations of the Posse Comitatus Act occur when the military is used to execute the law.[232] Often, as was the case in *Dreyer*, the military violates the Posse Comitatus Act without the request or assistance of law enforcement.[233] Civilian law enforcement obtained a search warrant, arrested, charged, and prosecuted Dreyer only after the military violated the Posse Comitatus Act—no civilian law enforcement official requested the military to execute the law.[234] Therefore, the courts should not punish civilian authorities when the military violates the law.

Excluding evidence will not deter future military misconduct. In *Dreyer*, the military turned illegally obtained evidence over to civilian law enforcement because it had no connection to the military. Since the military did not have an interest in the prosecution of the case, excluding the evidence would not impact the military. Using the exclusionary rule in a civilian prosecution does not deter future military misconduct. Excluding evidence would punish civilian law enforcement for the misdeeds of the military even though civilian law enforcement never participated or requested the improper military actions. Since the actions were done by the military, civilian law enforcement cannot be deterred by the exclusion of evidence. Since the prosecution is by civilians, it is unlikely that the military will be deterred from future conduct that violates the Posse Comitatus Act. Therefore, excluding evidence is not an effective deterrent.

Criminal punishment for those who misuse the military is an effective deterrent. Military commanders who use the military for domestic law enforcement can be sent to prison and fined. Although criminal prosecutions of military commanders are very rare, the mere fact that a commander could face prison can cause the commander to refrain from unlawful conduct. This is a significant deterrent, and the courts should respect the legislative process by refusing to add additional sanctions. It is Congress's role to decide what the appropriate punishment is for the statutes that it enacts.

---

[232] *See* 18 U.S.C. § 1385 (2016).
[233] United States v. Dreyer, 804 F.3d 1266, 1270 (9th Cir. 2015) (*en banc*).
[234] *Id.* at 1270–71.

VI. CONCLUSION

The Supreme Court has struggled with the proper application of the judicially created exclusionary rule, and the Court has restricted its application in recent years. The exclusionary rule should be used in limited circumstances when police violate the Constitution, and when excluding the evidence gained through a constitutional violation would deter future police misconduct.[235] The Posse Comitatus Act criminalizes the use of the military to execute the law, and deters misuse of the military through criminal sanctions.[236] Both the exclusionary rule and the Posse Comitatus Act are deeply rooted in U.S. history, and both were created to ensure that government officials act in ways that protect civil liberties. However, these doctrines must not be mixed. The exclusionary rule should not be applied to exclude evidence derived from a violation of the Posse Comitatus Act.

---

[235] *See* Davis v. United States, 564 U.S. 229, 236–38 (2011) (citing Hudson v. Michigan, 547 U.S. 586, 596 (2006)).
[236] 18 U.S.C. § 1385.

How Cybersecurity Regulation for the Smart Grid Could Upset the Current Balance of Federal and State Jurisdiction in Electricity Regulation

Cynthia Anderson*

I. INTRODUCTION

It is a truism to say that electricity is integral to modern life, from the basic uses of providing light and heating to the more modern economic necessity of the Internet. A widespread or long-term electric grid failure would devastate the United States.[1] Despite continually growing reliance, significant efforts to upgrade the grid and take advantage of new technologies with the potential to transform grid efficiency and reliability have only been underway for about the last decade.[2] In the United States, there is a coordinated effort between the

---

* **Cynthia Anderson** is currently a judicial law clerk and will soon transition to an attorney-advisor role in the United States government. She holds a JD, *magna cum laude*, from American University Washington College of Law (2016) and a BA in business administration from Oregon State University (2009).

[1] Robert Miller, *Hurricane Katrina: Communications & Infrastructure Impacts*, in THREATS AT OUR THRESHOLD: HOMELAND DEFENSE AND HOMELAND SECURITY IN THE NEW CENTURY 191, 191 (Bert B. Tussing ed., 2006), http://cisac.fsi.stanford.edu/sites/default/files/071022_ThreatsAtOurThreshold.pdf (describing the collapse of critical infrastructure, including the electrical grid, as "catastrophic").
[2] The main legislation directing resources towards the Smart Grid was enacted in December 2007. *See* Energy Independence and Security Act of 2007, Pub. L. No. 110-140

federal and state governments and the private sector to implement these technologies, creating what is referred to as the Smart Grid.[3]

Despite a general agreement between the government, private industry, and academics to pursue the Smart Grid's implementation, basic arguments about how the technologies should be implemented, and whether the U.S. regulatory environment should be restructured, as a result, are still largely unresolved.[4] Under the current framework, each state retains regulatory authority over most aspects of electricity generation and all aspects of distribution, leaving a fairly limited role for the federal government.[5] Inherent in the design of the Smart Grid, however, is an increased interconnectedness that makes differing regulatory standards all the more likely to have a significant impact on broader grid reliability and interstate commerce.[6] This potential for grid-wide impact is nowhere more clear-cut than in relation to cybersecurity standards.[7]

(2007). The organization at "the forefront of research into the feasibility of the smart grid on a large scale" was established in 2008. EarthTalk, *How Upgrading the Power Grid Will Save Energy and Money*, SCIENTIFIC AMERICAN (Apr. 6, 2009), https://www.scientificamerican.com/article/upgrading-power-grid/# (discussing the Future Renewable Electric Energy Delivery and Management Systems Center and its work with "universities, industry and national laboratories" to develop smart technologies).

[3] *See* Joel B. Eisen, *Smart Regulation and Federalism for the Smart Grid*, 37 HARV. ENVTL. L. REV. 1, 6 (2013) (indicating that both federal and state governments have begun to build "[c]omprehensive policy frameworks").

[4] *See* discussion *infra* Part III (explaining competing views over regulatory structure of the Smart Grid).

[5] *See* discussion *infra* Section II.B (discussing traditional jurisdictional lines related to electricity regulation).

[6] *See* discussion *infra* Section II.C.ii.a (detailing concerns about the potential impact of the Smart Grid structure on the security of the electric grid).

[7] As this article went to press, information was released by the United States Computer Emergency Readiness Team ("US-CERT") that underscored the potential for a cybersecurity breach of the U.S. electric grid, and the need to ensure even the most remote portions of the grid are made secure. US-CERT revealed in an Alert released March 15, 2018, that the Russian Government had "targeted small commercial facilities' networks where they staged malware, conducted spear phishing, and gained remote access into energy sector networks. *See* Russian Government Cyber Activity Targeting Energy and Other Critical Infrastructure Sectors, TA18-074A (Mar. 15, 2018), https://www.us-cert.gov/ncas/alerts/TA18-074A. Although the information was

State governments and many local utilities argue that implementing the Smart Grid should not have any effect on the jurisdictional balance between the states and the federal government.[8] While this is largely accepted in relation to rate-setting and utility-siting, many academics argue that federal jurisdiction should be expanded when setting cybersecurity standards to protect against potential vulnerabilities caused by differing standards.[9]

II. BACKGROUND

A. Overview of the Electrical Grid Structure

In the United States, the electrical grid is separated into two regional interconnections and three intrastate grids.[10] The Eastern Interconnection is comprised of all of the states east of the Rockies, and portions of Canada.[11] The Western Interconnection is comprised of all of the contiguous states west of the Rockies, and portions of Canada and

---

recently publicized, the Russian government has been targeting U.S. critical infrastructure since at least March 2016. *Id.*

[8] *See* Eisen, *supra* note 3, at 51 (saying that "[s]tates are virtually unwilling to cede any authority to [the Federal Energy Regulatory Commission]" when it comes to regulating the Smart Grid).

[9] *See* discussion *infra* Section II.B (citing academic articles arguing that federal regulation is necessary).

[10] *See Learn More About Interconnections,* OFFICE OF ELECTRICITY DELIVERY & ENERGY RELIABILITY, U.S. DEP'T OF ENERGY, http://energy.gov/oe/services/electricity-policy-coordination-and-implementation/transmission-planning/recovery-act-0 (last visited Apr. 10, 2018) [hereinafter *Learn More*] (describing the Eastern and Western Interconnections and recognizing Alaska and most of Texas as having discrete grids); William Pentland, *What is at Stake for Hawaii in NextEra Energy – HECO Merger,* FORBES (Jan. 30, 2015), http://www.forbes.com/sites/williampentland/2015/01/30/what-is-at-stake-for-hawaii-in-nextera-energy-heco-merger/ (recognizing that Hawaii, Alaska, and Texas are run separate from the regional grids due, in the case of the former two, to physical isolation).

[11] *See Learn More, supra* note 9 (recognizing that most of Texas is excluded from the Eastern Interconnection).

Mexico.[12] Because the regional interconnections involve the interstate transmission of electricity, federal jurisdiction to regulate is implicated in certain parts of the process, as described below.[13]

There are three distinct components to the electrical grid for regulatory purposes—generation, transmission, and distribution.[14] Electricity generation occurs at individual, intrastate plants utilizing a variety of methods, including coal-burning, nuclear reaction, and solar conversion.[15] Generated electricity is routed through high-power, intrastate voltage lines for transmission to meet usage needs across the entire interconnection.[16] While bulk electricity sales do occur directly among providers along the high-voltage transmission lines, final distribution to end consumers such as businesses and individual homes is facilitated by local utility companies.[17] Despite the integrated ability to transmit power generated in one state to an end user in another, providers have had limited visibility into issues along the grid.[18] Representative of this limited visibility is the fact that "utilit[ies] often only know[] where an outage is located when [they] receive[] a customer's phone call."[19]

---

[12] *Id.* Note, although the Eastern and Western Interconnections both extend beyond the boundaries of the United States, that does not change anything discussed below regarding jurisdictional authority.

[13] *See* discussion *infra* Section I.B (describing the existing federal and state jurisdictional boundaries). Note that because their grids are contained wholly within the borders of one state, Hawaii, Alaska, and the majority of Texas are not subject to federal jurisdiction and are thus outside of the scope of this paper. *See* Pentland, *supra* note 9.

[14] *See, e.g.*, New York v. Fed. Energy Reg. Comm'n, 535 U.S. 1, 5–6 (2002) [hereinafter *New York v. FERC*] (recognizing generation, transmission, and distribution as fundamental aspects of providing electricity and that Congress drew jurisdictional lines along those three categories in the Federal Power Act ("FPA") of 1935).

[15] Ashira Pelman Ostrow, *Grid Governance: The Role of a National Network Coordinator*, 35 CARDOZO L. REV. 1993, 2001 (2014).

[16] *See id.* (explaining that transmission networks have been increasingly interconnected to increase grid reliability and defray costs of expensive new power plants through co-ownership).

[17] *See New York v. FERC*, 535 U.S. at 10–11 (recognizing that transmission lines are integral to the bulk power market but that sales to retail customers occur through state-regulated utility companies).

[18] *See* Eisen, *supra* note 3, at 8 (noting a general failure to use sensors and other technology for monitoring).

[19] *Id.*

B. Federal and State Jurisdictional Lines in Electricity Regulation

Federal jurisdiction over the electrical grid is derived from Congress's constitutional authority to regulate interstate commerce.[20] Regulatory authority is, therefore, divided between the state and federal governments based on whether the function of an action or regulated entity is intrastate or interstate in nature. Jurisdictional boundaries have essentially followed those established by Congress under the Federal Power Act of 1935 ("FPA").[21]

The FPA provides for federal jurisdiction over the transmission and wholesale sale of electric energy in interstate commerce.[22] It specifically exempts from federal jurisdiction any facilities used in electricity generation, local distribution, and intrastate transmission.[23] Thus, of the three components of the electrical grid, only transactions associated with high-voltage interstate transmission lines fall under the *general* jurisdiction of the Federal Energy Regulatory Commission ("FERC").

Although FERC only has general authority to regulate interstate transmission and wholesale sales, it does have limited jurisdiction over electricity generation facilities. The Energy Policy Act of 2005 amended the FPA to extend federal jurisdiction over "generation facilities needed to maintain transmission system reliability" for purposes of mandatory grid reliability standards affecting interstate transmission and the bulk-power system.[24] Accordingly, the federal government has *some* form of regulatory authority over two of the three components of the electrical grid.

---

[20] *See, e.g., New York v. FERC*, 535 U.S. at 5–6 (explaining that the Federal Power Act of 1935 was enacted to provide for federal regulation over aspects of the electrical grid that states could not regulate under the Commerce Clause).

[21] *See* Christopher Bosch, Note, *Securing the Smart Grid: Protecting National Security and Privacy Through Mandatory, Enforceable Interoperability Standards*, 41 FORDHAM URB. L.J. 1349, 1398 (2014) (noting that the FPA provided the original statutory basis for federal regulation of the electric grid, though the scope of allowed regulation has grown over time due to increased interconnectedness of the grid).

[22] 16 U.S.C. § 824(a) (2014).

[23] *Id.* § 824(b)(1).

[24] *Id.* § 824o(a)(1)(B); *see also id.* at § 824o(b) (defining commission jurisdiction).

Though there is no explicit statutory authority for federal regulation of distribution-level public utilities, some voluntary actions by the utilities can bring them under FERC jurisdiction for rate-setting purposes. In *New York v. FERC*,[25] the Supreme Court reviewed FERC Order No. 888, which, *inter alia*, required application of a single tariff for all utilities purchasing transmission services whenever retail utilities voluntarily unbundled generation and transmission pricing.[26] New York argued that FERC had exceeded the boundaries of its jurisdiction in attempting to regulate unbundled retail transmission prices because all retail transactions were "properly the subject of state regulation."[27] The Supreme Court rejected New York's argument, however, and concluded that FERC did have jurisdiction to regulate the unbundled retail transmission of electricity because it had jurisdiction over any transmission in interstate commerce and "the nature of the national grid" results in all electricity transmission being aggregated on the same transmission lines.[28]

C. The Smart Grid

The Smart Grid is a coordinated effort across the electricity industry to create "robust communication paths between end-use consumers . . . and upstream to the utilities, or other energy service providers."[29] There are five categories of Smart Grid systems being implemented[30]:

---

[25] *New York v. FERC*, 535 U.S. 1.
[26] *Id.* at 11.
[27] *Id.* at 16.
[28] *Id.* at 17. *See id.* at 7, 17, 20 (reviewing the structure of the electrical grid and concluding that transmission was inherently interstate in nature and therefore properly subject to federal regulation, regardless of whether the end purchaser was wholesale or retail).
[29] Ray Gifford & Eric Gunning, *Telecommunications & Electronic Media: The Opportunity and Peril of Smart Grid*, 11 ENGAGE 128 (2010).
[30] *See* U.S. GOV'T ACCOUNTABILITY OFFICE, GAO-11-117, ELECTRICITY GRID MODERNIZATION: PROGRESS BEING MADE ON CYBERSECURITY GUIDELINES, BUT KEY CHALLENGES REMAIN TO BE ADDRESSED 7 tbl.1 (2011) [hereinafter "GAO Report"] (explaining the Smart Grid system categories described by the National Energy Technology Laboratory ("NETL")).

(1) Integrated communications;[31] (2) advanced components;[32] (3) advanced control methods;[33] (4) sensing and measurement;[34] and (5) improved interfaces and decision support.[35] The U.S. Department of Energy lists the following anticipated benefits of the Smart Grid technologies include:

- More efficient transmission of electricity
- Quicker restoration of electricity after power disturbances
- Reduced operations and management costs for utilities, and ultimately lower power costs for consumers
- Reduced peak demand, which will also help lower electricity rates
- Increased integration of large-scale renewable energy systems
- Better integration of customer-owner power generation systems, including renewable energy systems
- Improved security[36]

---

[31] Integrated communication systems are "[h]igh-speed, fully integrated, two-way communications technologies" that allow for "real-time information and power exchange." *Id.* These technologies are implemented along the distribution channels or in consumer homes. *Id.*

[32] Advanced component systems utilize the latest technologies to "produce higher power densities, greater reliability and power quality . . . and improved real-time diagnostics." *Id.* Examples include enhanced use of storage devices, "smart appliances" in consumer homes and businesses, and local "microgrids" that can operate independently from the larger grid when necessary. *Id.*

[33] Advanced control methods systems "monitor power system components" to "improve utilization of generation and transmission assets" by, for instance, using sensors along substation and distribution facilities to automatically identify system failures. *Id.* at 8.

[34] Sensing and measurement systems provide information about equipment functionality and consumer demand to utility companies and inform consumers about current prices and demand. *Id.* This is accomplished through use of "smart meters," sensors, "[c]onsumer portals," and "[d]ynamic line-rating devices." *Id.*

[35] Improved interface and decision support systems utilize software to analyze system data and enable utility employees to make "more accurate and timely" decisions. *Id.*

[36] OFFICE OF ELECTRICITY DELIVERY & ENERGY RELIABILITY, U.S. DEP'T OF ENERGY, *What is the Smart Grid?*, SMARTGRID.GOV, https://www.smartgrid.gov/the_smart_grid/smart _grid.html (last visited Apr. 10, 2018).

i. Energy Independence and Security Act of 2007

While efforts were initiated by private industry, both federal and state legislators have taken steps to promote the initiative.[37] The primary federal statute regulating Smart Grid progress is the Energy Independence and Security Act of 2007 ("EISA").[38] EISA lays out ten goals for the Smart Grid that, together, are intended to "maintain a reliable and secure electricity infrastructure that can meet future demand growth . . . ."[39] Additionally, it provides direction for the creation of a uniform framework of interoperability standards that will ensure all components of the Smart Grid can interact effectively and securely.[40] In doing so, it provides for some additional federal jurisdiction over the electricity industry.[41]

EISA assigns the National Institute of Standards and Technology ("NIST") primary responsibility for coordinating the development of a framework of interoperability standards for the Smart Grid.[42] It requires NIST to solicit input from other federal committees, including the Smart Grid Task Force and the Smart Grid Advisory Committee,[43] as well as state agencies and private industry.[44] The NIST standards

---

[37] *See* GAO Report, *supra* note 29, at 4 (acknowledging that electricity industry made initial steps towards updating the grid to take advantage of new technologies); Eisen, *supra* note 3, at 6 (indicating that both federal and state governments have begun to build "[c]omprehensive policy frameworks").

[38] *See* Eisen, *supra* note 3, at 5 (explaining that Congress enacted EISA to prescribe the Smart Grid standards-setting process).

[39] 42 U.S.C. § 17381 (2014). EISA's ten listed goals for the Smart Grid system inform the work conducted by the NETL and the National Institute of Standards and Technology ("NIST") as described *supra* notes 21–26 and accompanying text.

[40] 42 U.S.C. § 17385(a)–(b) (2012).

[41] *See* discussion *infra* Section II.C.i (describing EISA-based federal jurisdiction).

[42] 42 U.S.C. § 17385(a).

[43] *Id.* § 17383(a)(1). The Smart Grid Task Force and Smart Grid Advisory Committee were established under EISA to act in an advisory capacity to relevant federal agency heads by being involved in federal, state, and private Smart Grid initiatives. *See* Energy Independence and Security Act of 2007, Pub. L. No. 110-140, 121 Stat. 1492 § 1303 (2007).

[44] 42 U.S.C. § 17385(a)(1)–(2).

are required to be "flexible, uniform and technology neutral."[45] However, state and industry adoption of the NIST standards is strictly voluntary.[46]

Under EISA, FERC is provided with jurisdiction to adopt NIST interoperability standards as mandatory through rulemaking proceedings where there is "sufficient consensus" regarding the standard, and it is "necessary to insure smart-grid functionality and interoperability in interstate transmission of electric power, and regional and wholesale electricity markets."[47] FERC has interpreted the language to mean that it has authorization to conduct rulemaking proceedings affecting distribution-level facilities, if necessary.[48] However, it is generally accepted that because EISA does not provide FERC with any additional enforcement authority, the standards will only be mandatory where they fall within FERC's other grants of jurisdictional authority under the FPA, as amended.[49]

ii. Cybersecurity Concerns

a. Identified Potential Vulnerabilities

In a 2011 report, the Government Accountability Office ("GAO") identified a number of potential vulnerabilities in the Smart Grid system.[50] The vulnerabilities included a larger number of potential entry points into the electrical grid by hackers as a result of increased integration

---

[45] *Id.* § 17385(b).
[46] *See* Bosch, *supra* note 20, at 1380–81 (explaining that NIST standards can only become mandatory if adopted through a FERC rulemaking proceeding in compliance with EISA requirements).
[47] 42 U.S.C. § 17385(d).
[48] *See* GAO Report, *supra* note 29, at 13 n.12.
[49] *Compare* GAO Report, *supra* note 29, at 18–19 (explaining that FERC would have the ability to enforce standards, in conjunction with the North American Electric Corporation, under its grid-reliability authorities and through incentive-based programs), *with* Eisen, *supra* note 3, at 37 (noting that FERC enforcement power is limited to "its existing FPA authorities to regulate interstate transmission of electricity").
[50] These vulnerabilities are reflected in the introductory "What GAO Found" section of the GAO Report. *See* GAO Report, *supra* note 29.

of grid components and newly implemented systems; unknown vulnerabilities inherent with new system and network technologies; the ability for hackers to affect a larger area of the grid at one time through interconnecting systems; and increased incentives to hack the system for monetary gain because of the potentially large amount of customer information stored within the system.[51] It is generally acknowledged that a single attack has the potential to cause region-wide electrical grid failures that could last for days at a time.[52] Such an occurrence could have an almost unimaginable economic and human impact, especially if a cyber-attack were coordinated with a physical terrorist attack.[53] As one commentator notes, the negative consequences of a widespread power outage are exacerbated by the interdependent nature of the nation's critical infrastructure systems, such as water and transportation, with the electrical grid.[54]

b. Attacks That Have Already Occurred

The GAO vaguely references a variety of cybersecurity issues that have already occurred or been proven to be a threat, in the United States and abroad.[55] Cybersecurity experts have shown that vulnerabilities in smart meters have the potential to allow a hacker to disrupt the electricity grid,[56] and the Central Intelligence Agency ("CIA") has

---

[51] *Id.* at 9 (listing categories of risk involving physical infrastructure).

[52] *E.g.*, Zhen Zhang, *Cybersecurity Policy for the Electricity Sector: The First Step to Protecting our Critical Infrastructure from Cyber Threats*, 19 B.U. J. SCI. & TECH. L. 319, 326–27 (2013) (discussing the means by which an attack may have wide reaching regional consequences).

[53] *Cf.* Miller, *supra* note 1 (describing the collapse of critical infrastructure, including the electrical grid, as "catastrophic").

[54] *See* Michael McElfresh, *Can the Smart Grid Survive a Cyberattack?*, ENERGY POST (June 29, 2015), http://www.energypost.eu/can-smart-grid-survive-cyberattack/ (quoting a report that called the electrical grid an obvious target for those seeking to do physical, economic and psychological harm to the nation).

[55] *See* GAO Report, *supra* note 29. The summary "What GAO Found" section acknowledges that the report was not able to adequately address the risk of attacks, despite the GAO's intention to do so.

[56] *See* Eduard Kovacs, *Smart Meters Pose Security Risks to Consumers, Utilities: Researcher*, SECURITY WEEK (Jan. 4, 2017), http://www.securityweek.com/smart-meters-pose-security-risks-consumers-utilities-researcher (explaining that hackers could hijack network traffic-connecting smart appliances and the grid and take control of devices).

already reported regional overseas power disruption as a result of "malicious activities against IT systems[.]"[57] The cited materials referencing the CIA-acknowledged attacks are no longer accessible, but there are still media reports available online. Though the media reports do not include specifics, one attack apparently resulted in a multi-city power failure, while others resulted in extortion demands.[58] The Stuxnet computer worm is also cited as an example of a significant cybersecurity concern for the U.S. electrical grid, though that attack was not carried out against an electrical grid.[59]

III. ARGUMENTS FOR AND AGAINST EXTENDING FEDERAL JURISDICTION

The arguments are fairly predictable for why or why not to extend federal jurisdiction over the electrical grid for cybersecurity standard-setting purposes. State regulators want to maintain the existing jurisdictional boundaries, which would keep federal involvement limited to aspects involving interstate transmission and wholesale sales.[60] Many academics argue, however, that it is necessary for federal jurisdiction to extend over the entire electrical grid for cybersecurity standard-setting purposes, to ensure consistency and compliance.[61] Each of these arguments contains additional nuance, explored further below.

Researchers have said that the security vulnerabilities have persisted, despite initial studies showing their existence in 2010. *Id.*

[57] *See* GAO Report, *supra* note 29, at 10.

[58] Tom Espiner, *CIA: Cyberattack Caused Multiple-City Blackout*, CNET NEWS (Jan. 22, 2008), https://www.cnet.com/news/cia-cyberattack-caused-multiple-city-blackout/.

[59] *See* McElfresh, *supra* note 53 (explaining how the systems used to operate the Smart Grid are substantially similar to those that were compromised by the Stuxnet computer worm, which shut down Iranian centrifuges used for uranium enrichment); Doug Drinkwater, *Stuxnet-style Attack on US Smart Grid Could Cost Government $1 Trillion*, SC MAGAZINE (July 13, 2015), http://www.scmagazineuk.com/stuxnet-style-attack-on-us-smart-grid-could-cost-government-1-trillion/article/426108/ (discussing a report that detailed why the U.S. electrical grid could be vulnerable to a Stuxnet-style attack).

[60] *E.g.*, Gifford & Gunning, *supra* note 28, at 130.

[61] *See* Bosch, *supra* note 20, at 1391–94 (explaining that voluntary or limited standards are insufficient because of the high stakes involved if a failure does occur).

A. Arguments for Maintaining Existing Jurisdictional Boundaries

There are essentially two categories of arguments for maintaining existing jurisdictional boundaries between state and federal governments for purposes of Smart Grid cybersecurity regulation: first, that the federal government only has enforcement authority over interstate transmission, and any further standards could only be enforced by influencing the states; and second, that there are practical concerns with mandating standards at a federal level.

It is noted that, even if FERC could mandate standards for all portions of the grid and all participants, "it [is] not clear how it would enforce a mandate."[62] Some argue that FERC "can only mandate standards for interstate transmission" and that it has no "authority over generation, middle-mile and last-mile distribution, or in-home energy management."[63] This traditional breakdown should continue to be seen in the jurisdictional boundaries for physical Smart Grid investments.[64] Thus, an attempt by the federal government to change its jurisdiction over Smart Grid cybersecurity could be seen by states as "an attempt to usurp some of the state powers with respect to the prudence of grid investments, interoperability mandates, and grid management."[65] Rather, it is necessary for federal agencies to convince states to enact the standards proposed by NIST in order to avoid legal challenges to federal jurisdictional authority.[66]

There are numerous practical concerns about a change in jurisdictional boundaries relating to cybersecurity of the Smart Grid. Specifically, the concerns relate to the potential negative effects of

---

[62] Eisen, *supra* note 3, at 51.
[63] Gifford & Gunning, *supra* note 28, at 129.
[64] *See id.* at 130 (discussing the juxtaposition between federal jurisdiction asserted over all cybersecurity of the smart grid with the retained traditional jurisdictional boundaries for physical infrastructure investment approvals).
[65] *Id.*
[66] *See* Resolution, Nat'l Ass'n of Reg. Util. Commissioners, Resolution Regarding Smart Grid (July 22, 2009), https://pubs.naruc.org/pub.cfm?id=53985C5D-2354-D714-51F0-F9226449 C37D (emphasizing the need for the federal government to partner with the state regulatory authorities in creating policies and standards for the Smart Grid and emphasizing jurisdictional lines for FERC and the state governments).

mandatory regulation.[67] For instance, private-sector commentators noted that it prefers voluntary standards because they are more flexible and less likely to be set arbitrarily or to remain in place despite becoming obsolete.[68] State governments and electricity providers expressed concern that any mandatory rules, even if limited to areas of traditional jurisdiction, would "gain traction and work their way down to the local level."[69] Thus, in effect, any federal rules would become the standard across all levels and undermine state authority to regulate.[70]

B. Arguments for Extending Federal Jurisdiction to Include Cybersecurity of all Aspects of the Smart Grid

Even proponents of extending FERC's jurisdiction do not assert that its enforcement authority was affected by EISA.[71] Rather, the arguments rest on the fact that FERC and the North American Electric Reliability Corporation ("NERC") can, in fact, promulgate rules under those acts—enforcement concerns aside—and that mandatory rules are simply necessary.[72] One reason why mandatory standards across the entire grid are necessary is that a grid failure would have such devastating consequences.[73] For instance, the aggregate impact of

---

[67] See Eisen, *supra* note 3, at 51 (identifying mandatory regulations as one of the greatest concerns for Smart Grid commentators).

[68] See *id.* at 51–52. (expressing concerns about mandatory FERC requirements and potential monopolization of the energy sector).

[69] *Id.* at 51.

[70] Cf. ROGER LEVY ET AL., SMART GRID STANDARDS: IMPLICATIONS FOR STATE REGULATORY COMMISSIONS; BACKGROUND AND FREQUENTLY ASKED QUESTIONS 13 (Nov. 2010), https://emp.lbl.gov/sites/default/files/naruc-nist111010.pdf (noting the potential for federal agency adoption to create jurisdictional issues while asserting that adoption of mandatory standards by some states could impact operations in other states in the interconnection).

[71] See Bosch, *supra* note 20, at 1392–93 (noting that EISA was unclear about how FERC would enforce the standards it allowed FERC to promulgate via rulemaking, but that FERC did not interpret its enforcement authorities to have been modified by the statute).

[72] See *id.* at 1393 (listing industry concerns resulting from a lacking standard).

[73] See *id.* at 1394 (emphasizing electricity's significant role in daily lives); *see also supra* notes 41–47 and accompanying text.

"smart grid home device[s]" on the bulk power grid could result in wide-spread reliability or security issues across an interconnection.[74] In addition, proponents argue that, rather than being negative for the industry by risking stagnant standards, a uniform approach would benefit stakeholders by providing certainty that investments into security and infrastructure will comply with requirements and thus industry stakeholders will not "risk losing their entire investment if future laws invalidate their approach."[75]

IV. CONCLUSION

Cybersecurity of the Smart Grid presents a unique problem regarding decades-old and long-settled jurisdictional boundaries in the area of electricity regulation. Because vulnerabilities at a single point on the Smart Grid could result in power failure on an interstate or regional scale, the concept of local distribution of power does not apply as directly as it would in traditional transactions. Though Congress has passed a law that does provide FERC with authority to promulgate rules-setting standards for cybersecurity of the Smart Grid, there remains controversy over whether, and to what extent, federal jurisdiction has been or should be broadened.

Industry commentators argue that mandatory rules set by the federal government will often be behind the curve on what is technologically possible and will be left in place long after becoming obsolete. Thus, the Smart Grid would inherently have unnecessary vulnerabilities that would be addressed by using the most up-to-date knowledge and technologies. On the other hand, proponents of expanding federal jurisdiction point out that whenever standards are not mandatory, some actors will always fail to implement necessary

---

[74] North American Electric Reliability Corporation, Comment of the North American Electric Reliability Corporation in Response to the Commission's March 19, 2009 Proposed Smart Grid Policy Statement 11 (May 11, 2009), http://www.nerc.com/files/NERCSmartGridPolicy StatementComments.pdf.

[75] *See* Bosch, *supra* note 20, at 1396–97 (quoting BOB LOCKHART & BOB GOHN, PIKE RESEARCH, UTILITY CYBER SECURITY: SEVEN KEY SMART GRID SECURITY TRENDS TO WATCH IN 2012 AND BEYOND 5 (2011)) (describing how uncertainty about standards at early stages is likely preventing investment and innovation).

safeguards. Because of the interconnected nature of the Smart Grid, any single vulnerability would have far-reaching consequences. Thus, a uniform approach would benefit stakeholders by providing clear guidance that supports investment in costly infrastructure and technology upgrades.

www.ingramcontent.com/pod-product-compliance
Lightning Source LLC
Chambersburg PA
CBHW070414230526
45471CB00006B/2801